WHAT PEOPLE ARE
THINGS:

"In a world where women are pulled in so many directions, *Simple Things* encourages us to let go of the chaos and focus on what is really important. Suzanne's words gently challenge the reader to take a deep breath and be herself while purposefully pointing our hearts toward a deeper intimacy with Christ. Perfect for a quick daily read or curling up with a favorite blanket and hot drink and settling in for a quiet moment of reflection, *Simple Things* reminds us to come to the Father to simply BE loved!"

-Liz Hoffman, Children's Resource Coordinator for the Illinois District of the Assemblies of God

"We all long for a simpler way. But living 'life'...can it really be simple? *Simple Things* is an engaging compilation that made me examine and consider my own life; and its complex simplicity. Suzanne's heart, and her passion for people and life is evident in each chapter. She challenged me to focus on the simple, and to be better; I'm certain the same will happen for you. I will definitely use *Simple Things* as a study with some girlfriends who need to hear its message. Thanks Suzanne!"

-Sonya Wilson, pastor's wife, speaker, teacher, and mentor.

"In *Simple Things* Suzanne reveals the wisdom that she has gleaned through the years in her "secrets"--really just practical advice for living as Jesus wants us to live.

Her humor and down-to-earth openness are refreshing, enlightening, and will encourage anyone who reads this book. Recommended for women of all walks of life whether in ministry or not."

-Doree Donaldson, Convoy:Women, Director. A division of Convoy of Hope

"Sometimes the simplest pleasures in life give us the greatest joy. In *Simple Things,* Suzanne Schaffer challenges us to return to the simple practices and values that restore our souls. Reading her humor and encouragement is like sitting down on the front porch with your best friend. She makes you feel at home."

-Leigh Powers, Author of *Renewed: A 40-Day Devotional for Healing from Church Hurt and for Loving Well in Ministry*

"Suzanne addresses Christianity just where it needs to be, in the simple things. While it can be easy to make following Jesus complicated, *Simple Things* gets back to the basics of your relationship with God and your relationship with the people in your life. Sharing Scripture, life experiences and even recipes (can't wait to try the brownies), Suzanne expresses her desire to follow Christ in a simple, everyday lifestyle."

-Marjie Tourville, Pastor's Wife and assistant to Dr. Stephen Tourville, Superintendent of the PennDel Ministry Network of the Assemblies of God

"What Suzanne Schaffer has accomplished in writing, *Simple Things* is nothing short of genius. She has taken several relevant topics within the circle of the Christian faith, and brought them to light with thoughtful prose and fun stories. What made reading this book particularly delightful were the elements of fun that Suzanne has woven into each chapter, whether by relatable stories or fantastic recipes. I found her voice straightforward and refreshing, like a cool glass of iced tea on a hot summer day. After reading many of the chapters I was aware Suzanne's words had taught me something that I could put into practice.

Do yourself a favor, don't only buy this book, but read it, cover to cover."

-Nicole Bingaman, author of *Falling Away from You*

"Sometimes it's the simple things that make all the difference in our lives. In this book, Suzanne uses humor, personal experiences, and practical Biblical wisdom to help us become the women of God we want to be—the women God designed us to be. As you read this book you'll feel like you're discussing real-life issues with a friend. So grab a cup of tea, get comfortable, and enjoy *Simple Things*."

-Adessa Holden, Woman's Minister and Author *Finding Healing* and *Finding Significance*

Simple Things

Suzanne Schaffer

Design: Marshall/Ferguson

Subject Headings: 1. Christian life 2. Women's Issues 3. Spiritual formation.

ISBN 978-0-692-89521-4 (paperback)
ISBN Kindle 978-0-692-89522-1 (ebook)
Printed in the United States of America

CONTENTS

Introduction

"It was a perfect day," Natalie scribbled into her journal. *"Spent the afternoon on the porch with the kids who didn't fight. Enjoyed a picnic dinner complete with fresh-squeezed lemonade, hubby's famous steaks on the grill, and a big piece of chocolate cake I didn't have to share. The phone didn't ring, and the only visitor was the mailman when he brought my Amazon order."*

Good thing she wrote it down because here comes tomorrow.

Natalie's full coffee cup fell and shattered, staining her white capris. The kids were *hangry*, and they wanted grandma's chicken soup, only grandma lives several states away. The house looked like Toys 'R Us vomited, and the baby gift delivered yesterday was duplicated at the shower today.

Welcome to real life. We can all relate to the tale in Natalie's journal, with good and bad days scattered among the pages. I have a plaque in my house that reads, *"Just when I was getting used to yesterday along came today."*

While everyone wants happily ever after, real life often plays out like the scene above, perhaps not all in one day; but I've lived enough to see this time and again. As Christians we were led to believe life would be different. Our days wouldn't be messy. However, life isn't a fairytale, and it sure isn't glamorous. Even the people we emulate in the Bible went through hard times, though we don't always see them written down. We see an overview of their lives, not their every day. Why is it hard to believe we share so much in common with them? If someone were to write an outline of your life, what would it say?

Would it repeat the mundane or highlight the extraordinary? I've told my husband my tombstone will read: *All she ever wanted was carlashes*, because he refuses to buy them for me, but that isn't reality.

I want my life summed up as, *She was faithful to God, and she delighted in His faithfulness to her,* because even on the messy days, He has always been there.

Life with God doesn't mean a carefree existence. We live in a crazy world with godless people. With Him by our side, we are able to navigate reality without losing hope. He provides peace in the middle of real life. When things are scattered and chaotic, God is a steadiness we can trust. He is constant and unchanging in a motion-filled world. We can over think the Christian life. People and ideas get in the way and blur our focus, which is this: live to please God, love Him, love people, and share His love with others. There isn't much we can change in our world, but we can influence our little corner of it by how we act and react.

As you read these pages, it's my hope that you find rest and laughter, learn from my mistakes, and grow in your walk with the Lord. Let's rediscover the simple things in a world where everything is complicated.

Questions for Reflection:

Remember a perfect day that you had. What made it special?

Now think about a bad day. How did you react to the bad things that happened?

What do you want to be remembered for?

-1-

Secrets, Part 1

Wayne and I married in January of 1992 and entered the world of full-time ministry in August of the same year. We have spent the past few decades learning more about life and ministry than was ever taught us in a classroom. These are some things I've learned along the way.

Secret #1
Laughter is a good thing.

"A cheerful heart is good medicine, but a crushed spirit dries up the bones." Proverbs 17:22 (NIV)

Laughter shouldn't be a secret, yet it seems people have forgotten how to laugh. Grumpy Cat, a celebrity feline, gained fame and an internet presence for her eternal sourpuss face and, while endearing on her, it is not so endearing on the face of those attending "Grumpy Church."

We can busy ourselves with the work of the Lord yet forget to live, and living involves laughing. One "Grumpy Church" we served in frightened people away with their disgruntled ways. Attendance diminished, and joy was nowhere to be found. For where laughter is, joy is sure to be alongside. Laughter lightens moods and breaks down barriers between people. Laughter invites others to join in. Laughter embraces differences and helps us see ourselves as we are, flaws and all. Laughter can get you through the hard times in life.

As a pastor's wife, I have learned having a sense of humor is a gift from God. I couldn't make it through ministry life without it. Laughter reduces stress and burns calories. I would rather spend an hour laughing with a friend than walking on the treadmill (pass the chocolate please). And while laughter produces deep lines on our faces, each one is full of memories and moments to cherish. "I love these frown lines on my forehead," said no one ever.

Do you remember the last time you laughed out loud? I don't mean adding an LOL to something funny online, but a real laugh.

Laughter happens daily in my home, many times when I'm the only one in the house. Funny things are everywhere if we take time to notice them.

While reading online reviews for a lice treatment kit, I found one that read, *To get rid of life you need to see a doctor.* One letter made all the difference, and I laughed.

A classified ad stated a car for sale was in great condition and was *spacey.* I think the writer meant spacious or roomy, but she combined the two and out came spacey.

On a walk with a friend, we passed a house with garbage at the curb. I glanced at it and doubled back to take a picture of a box labeled, *Donated Human Tissue.* I posted the picture on Facebook with the caption, "What are they doing in that house?" I know it was probably just used to carry something home from work in, but that box made my mind run wild. Are they creating their own human in the basement out of donated parts? What parts were donated? Can I get new thighs there?

Funny has a way of sneaking up on me, often at inappropriate times. My husband officiated a funeral for an elderly woman we'd never met until she was lying in her casket. Funerals are not supposed to be funny; the mood is somber and the attendees are passing tissues.

On this day an elderly friend of the deceased was seated in the front, and she spent most of the service talking at a loud level. The lady sitting next to her would lean over and pat her hand, attempting to quiet her. The room grew silent as the daughters of the deceased stood to read a tribute to their mother. Front row lady started moaning during the tribute. "Oh, it hurts," she said, quietly at first, and then repeated it several times until all attention was on her. The tribute paused while she was helped to a standing position and slowly walked out of the room. As she was led away she kept talking, "It hurts. I have to get it out. I have to get the gas out."

The three daughters at the podium were wide-eyed. My husband purposefully avoided eye contact with me. The room was silent, save the moans of the exiting woman. Then I noticed a shoulder shaking in the row in front of me. I looked around and saw it was happening across the room, silent laughter took over and it felt good. It changed the mood and gave everyone in attendance something to remember about that day.

There are other times that the only thing I remember about the day is the funny thing that happened. One Sunday morning at the end of the church service, my husband and I made our way to the foyer to shake hands with the congregants as they were leaving. Shaking hands with people has never been a favorite activity of mine. I don't know where your hands have been and when they were last washed. A point made clear when a member of our congregation swiped her hand across her nose and then held it out for me to shake. My inner grimace stayed hidden under my forced smile.

On this same day another attendee named Janet made her way straight to me. In her late eighties, she often told me how much she loved my husband and how handsome he was. Her age and her walker didn't give me cause for concern. She wasn't one to quickly talk and leave, she had to grab my arm to make sure she had my full attention every time we spoke. It was winter and I chill easily, so I had on a black fleece cape.

Okay, it was a glorified blanket with a faux fur collar.

Janet grabbed my left arm and started talking to me, then let go and repeated the same with my right arm. I wasn't concentrating on what she was saying, but instead on what she was doing. When she walked away, I was caught up in laughter. My friend Liz approached to ask what had me so tickled. I told her that neither time had Janet been holding my arms. The cape was concealing, and to someone with questionable eyesight probably even

17

more so, but that was the first time I was ever woman-handled at church. I doubled over when Liz said, "Well, we really are a full-service church, aren't we?"

Another friend shared the following story with me: "I saw my husband across the room at our annual conference for pastors in our state. I walked up behind him and slipped my hand down, giving him a quick pinch on his behind. Imagine my surprise when he turned around and was not my spouse but another pastor."

This lady has a great sense of humor, and without it, may have been in self-induced solitary confinement for the rest of the conference. Laughter can help you get through the most awkward of circumstances. It is a gift God gave us, and it's okay to use it.

He gives us things to laugh at every day. This is the creator of the duck-billed platypus and the naked mole rat. If that isn't proof He has a sense of humor, I don't know what is. Go ahead and laugh. You'll feel better after you do it. Trust me.

Secret #2

The whole Bible is still relevant.

From beginning to end, Genesis to Revelation, the entire Bible is God-inspired and is still important. We can't pick and choose the pieces we like and discount the rest. The Bible can help you in your every day.

This shouldn't be a surprise to any of us. Those parts you don't like? The parts that make you feel uncomfortable? Perhaps God is trying to tell you something in those lines.

I have a love/hate relationship with the books Paul wrote. Similar to my love/hate relationship with my treadmill, I know it's good for me and I feel better after the work has been done, but it hurts and it's hard. Galatians, Ephesians, Philippians, and Colossians get me every time. I know I need to read and learn, but it makes me a little uncomfortable.

"Anyone who has been stealing must steal no longer, but must work, doing something useful with their own hands, that they may have something to share with those in need." Ephesians 4:28 (NIV)

I'm good there. No stealing going on here except for the spoonful of Nutella I didn't add into the MyFitnessPal app.

My husband thought I was napping on a recent Sunday afternoon until I confessed I'd been on the couch watching a Hallmark Channel movie with a jar of Nutella in one hand and a spoon in the other. Every girl has a weakness; mine is good chocolate.

I also steal glances at the hot guy I'm married to, and

I'll admit to stealing a kiss now and then. Otherwise, I'm good. No shoplifting mug shots. No pictures of me on the local police Facebook page asking for help in my identification. Not even a speeding ticket.

The second part of that verse doesn't worry me either, as a wife and a mother it seems all I do is work from sun up to sundown. That verse makes me feel good about myself. I can walk a little taller. God has just patted me on the head and smiled at me as I walk through this day, a conqueror.

Until I get to the next verse.

"Do not let any unwholesome talk come out of your mouths, but only what is helpful for building others up according to their needs, that it may benefit those who listen." Ephesians 4:29 (NIV)

I don't have a potty mouth. In fact, I'll be the one making the loud "blah blah blah" noises and covering the ears of children if someone is on an obscenity-laced rant in a public place. I don't curse or spew hate speech, but I have been known to mutter sarcastic thoughts and thoughtless words on occasion. The feeling I had when I read the previous verse has been replaced with shame. Are the words I mutter beneficial to others? I doubt it. When the car in front of me turns without using a turn signal, and I speak my displeasure by labeling them an idiot, am

I being a good example to the kids in the backseat? Am I pleasing God at that moment?

This is one example from two side-by-side verses in the Bible. The entire Bible is full of nuggets to help you be the person God wants you to be. Are you tired of the mundane? He has more for you. He loves you and only has your best interest in mind.

In our walk with the Lord we are to be continuously moving closer to Him and becoming more like Him in our thoughts and actions. Habits will change and give room for new ways of thinking and living. My husband has a habit of leaving things around the house. I don't mean the normal socks and underwear on the floor, but things like bottle caps, gum wrappers, and receipts. He will get a piece of gum from the cabinet and drop the wrapper on the table as he walks by, instead of throwing it in the closest trashcan. I come along later and pick it up. While it used to annoy me, I now laugh at his consistency.

For several months a Lowe's home improvement store receipt sat on the clothes dryer in the basement. I noticed it but never really saw it until I read it one day between laundry loads. The Lowe's tagline reads, "Never stop improving." That is exactly what we should be doing in our lives as Christians. His word, the entire Bible, is a guidebook to help us never stop improving, and it works as one cohesive thread, pulling words from the centuries, to show us how we can live a more rewarding life. When we make Him happy, we benefit, and the rewards are eternal.

Secret #3

Marriage is hard work.

If you've been married longer than a month, you know this isn't a secret. All around us are people who have tried marriage and failed, some numerous times. If it were easy, divorce wouldn't exist. It's almost as if we expect marriage to fail. I heard a newly engaged woman on the Grammy Red Carpet say, "This is my first wedding, and I don't know how to do it."

Do any of us know how to do it? I'm a quarter century into it and still am not sure I've got it right. When we vowed, "for richer or poorer," "in sickness and in health," "for better or for worse," we were mostly in for the richer, healthier and better parts. While it is full of these things, it is also full of the other ones, the ones we don't like to talk about. We put on happy faces and pretend we are living the fairytale. Most of what I learned about marriage and relationships as a teenager came from what I observed at home, on TV (courtesy of *Days of Our*

Lives), at the theater with 80's chick flicks starring Molly Ringwald, and in the semi-trashy romance novels I read but shouldn't have.

My newlywed expectations were of my husband doting on me and spending time doing the things I liked to do. I knew we would not spend our evenings in front of the television like other married couples. I knew he would give me flowers and chocolates every Valentine's Day and anniversary because that's what my dad did for my mom. We wouldn't argue much because we were best friends; just being together would be enough. I mean this is the guy who I would spend three hours on the phone with in the middle of the night while we were long-distancing between Phoenix and Pittsburgh. This was BC (before cell's) when we had to pay several hundred dollars a month for long distance calls. Surely he'd proven his affection for me, and in all those long talks we never argued.

Disney's *Enchanted* is one of my favorite movies. Giselle meanders through life in a haze where animals and birds talk to her. Everything in her world is perfect until she stumbles on an old man who robs her in the night. Even her gentle reaction of saying he isn't a very nice old man after he robs her, is the worst thing she can do. My expectations of marriage were fairytale-esque at best.

What I didn't realize is while I was growing up in the same house for eighteen years, attending the same Christian school for eight years, living just a few miles from my grandparents and visiting them weekly, the man I would marry was growing up quite differently. My Wayne is a PK (preacher's kid). He moved every few years and went to four different high schools. He lived hours from his grandparents and only saw them a few times a year. At one point we lived only a few miles away from each other yet were in different atmospheres.

"As the Scriptures say, "A man leaves his father and mother and is joined to his wife, and the two are united into one." Ephesians 5:31 (NLT)

The man I married is two days older than me. You might think we'd be somewhat alike being born so close together, but we are as opposite as can be. I go to bed early and rise with a smile and a song. He stays up late and doesn't want to speak until he's showered and dressed. I can sit quietly on the porch with a cup of tea and think deep thoughts for hours while he needs to be doing something. My idea of entertainment is *Arsenic and Old Lace* with Cary Grant, a Judy Garland musical, an Amy Grant concert, or checking out the new OPI shades at Ulta. He lives for football season so he can cheer on his Pittsburgh Steelers. We probably have more differences than similarities, and I had no idea two becoming one would take work.

Our first Thanksgiving together cemented how different we were. He's of Pennsylvania Dutch heritage, and I'm mostly Italian. On this day we traveled to his grandparent's house near Reading, PA where I found a tableful of dishes that I couldn't imagine the Pilgrims having served. Stewed dried corn, green bean casserole, cottage cheese and apple butter, shoo-fly pie, funny cake, birch beer, and Grammy's marshmallow puffs. As I looked at the spread, I wanted to cry. Where was the Italian bread and the real cranberries? Why is green bean casserole a thing? What on earth is birch beer? It wasn't wrong; it was different. Over time I came to appreciate the different. There is nothing like the wintergreen flavor of a fizzy birch beer soda. Shoo-fly pie is a molasses delight. I haven't made peace with the dried corn, but Wayne doesn't like the homemade cranberries I make room for on the table. I still can't figure out why green bean casserole exists, but marriage is about living and learning. Every day is new and different.

Who knew taking two people from different backgrounds and allowing them "to have and to hold" would be so hard? We didn't have reality shows to clue us in. My head was still filled with the romance novel idea of life. Our first few years were rocky at best. We learned to fight and to tune each other out. We learned to put on happy faces and pretend everything was normal. We learned what made the other angry and used it to our advantage. All of this while serving in full-time ministry.

We were able to hide what was going on from most everyone except for family. While neither of us had parents who interfered in our lives we were approached by some who thought perhaps a marriage retreat would help. They took our infant son and sent us off to a conference in Virginia Beach. We learned a lot that weekend and it was a turning point in our marriage. We realized it was okay to seek help and not something to be ashamed of. We are each imperfect, and we entered into a union where the church world expects everything to be rosy. It can take years to get to the place where two finally feel as one, but it's a daily commitment. There will be problems along the way. There will be little things that build into skyscrapers if you let them.

Wayne and I wandered through twenty-three years of marriage, fighting over which is the correct way to squeeze the toothpaste. I'm a squeeze and go brusher, and he is the one who squeezes the tube from one end and pushes it all to the other end. It always looked nice until I came along and did my thing. It bothered him more than me. We reached an impasse and decided to get our own *his* and *hers* toothpastes. What a simple solution. No more bathroom brawls over crushed Crest. We are free to squeeze as we wish. Not every squabble can be solved so easily; some take years and counselors, but it is worth it.

Can we talk for a minute about the other part of that verse? The "leave father and mother and cling to his wife" part?

I've seen many marriage relationships marred by the in-laws. When you marry and become one with your man, the two of you are a family unit. What you talk about, what you do, what you think of each other's parents, should stay between the two of you. Taking your mother's opinion over that of your husband's is not a good idea. Barring being mistreated or abused, please don't run to your parents when things aren't going your way. The two of you need to work on the problems you're having without getting other people involved. Your mother and father will usually side with you because they love you. The same goes for his parents.

There are other things we've had to work on. Wayne is a sports fan (read: all sports), and I am not a fan of any sport. Not. At. All. I've tried to attend games with him. The week I met him I played golf with him (hasn't happened since). The first time I went to a Penn State football game I watched everything but the game. As I write I can hear the sounds of football from the television in the other room, and it's making me a little crazy.

We've had to make an effort to find things to do together that we enjoy. Every week we spend a day I've dubbed *Date Day* together. We typically go to lunch because we enjoy eating out. It's important to spend time together on a regular basis because it builds a foundation for later years. We've dined around the world without traveling too far from home. Have you had Indian naan? Thai drunken noodles? We have access to an Eastern European grocery store that sells some of the best chocolate I've tasted. Bubble tea is something we tried together. We know where to get the best smoked chicken wings and we know which of the four Mexican restaurants in our town has the best tres leche cake. Together we've learned that falafel is awful and that we don't like salads made with iceberg lettuce. We visit local chocolate shops when we're on vacation and purchase a truffle or two just to see who has the best. We have rediscovered each other during these journeys through the food world.

We recently started attending auctions, and it has changed our lives. One word of warning though: if you take your husband to an auction, let him get his own bidding number. If he's competitive like Wayne, he will come home with enough paper towel dispensers and industrial toilet paper holders to re-do most of the bathrooms of the churches in your town and brag that it only cost him pocket change. Since attending auctions we've been able to redecorate our house, stock my online store, and spend time with people unrelated to our church, which provides a way to clear our minds of church-related stress.

You and your spouse may not be into dining out or attending auctions; those are our things. Find what you like to do together. There is a world of options.

Things You May Want to Try:

Bowling

Taking a class together

Renting bikes and exploring your favorite city

Playing board games or video games

Indulging in a couples massage

Making popcorn, spreading pillows on the floor, and having a Netflix marathon (you're married, you're totally allowed to *Netflix and chill*)

Going to a farmer's market

Reading a history book of your town together

Visiting the batting cages or driving range

Going to open houses

Volunteering together

Grocery shopping in a different store (trust me, it's fun)

Try your hand at geocaching

Taking a board game or a puzzle to a coffee shop

Ordering Chinese food for each other (try something different!)

Taking a gourmet picnic on a mountain hike

Visiting your closest state or national park

Hitting up the local tourist attractions (sometimes you live so close to them you never visit them)

Going to an amusement park

Going to your local high school's spring play

Visiting a pet store and marveling at all of the different fish God created

Adopting a dog and signing up for training classes

Going to a shooting range

Going to the zoo or aquarium

Visit another town close by and stay in an Air B&B

Going to opening day of your favorite baseball team

Attending a parade

Whatever you find to do, make sure you do it because it's important to spend time together. Write it on your calendar if you have to. If you are having trouble in your marriage, the problems will only worsen if you avoid each other. There will always be things you don't see eye to eye on. You are two different people with two different backgrounds. And just when you start getting used to each other, life happens. The cat gets hit by a car, the gas bill is four months behind and they are threatening to turn it off, the roof leaks, you get bad news from the doctor's office, rent is going up (again), squirrels have built a nest under the hood of your car, or a loved one has died. Life gets hard, and if you don't have a solid foundation during the easy times, then there will be nothing to carry you through the hard times together.

Life changes constantly, and you will need a lot of prayer to get through it.

Questions for Reflection:

When did you last laugh out loud?

Do funny things happen to you?

What nuggets have you gathered from the Bible?

Which parts of the Bible are the most challenging for you to read?

Which parts are easiest?

Are you married? Has it been easy? Have you had to work through tough things?

How has marriage changed your life?

In what ways have you had to change in order to grow in your marriage?

Grammy's Marshmallow Puffs

~A remembrance of my first Schaffer Thanksgiving

1 - 16 ounce bag regular size marshmallows
1 – 12 ounce package chocolate chips
½ cup creamy peanut butter
2 tablespoons butter

Melt the chocolate chips, peanut butter, and butter together in a saucepan over low heat.

Mix well and spread into an 8x8 pan.

Insert the marshmallows into the chocolate mixture until they are halfway down.

Refrigerate until set and then cut into squares and serve.

Store in refrigerator.

-2-

Zoey

We keep our dog tethered on a lead when she needs to go outside. It's not because we want to keep her from exploring her kingdom and chasing the squirrels, groundhogs, and rabbits that taunt her. It's because we know that just beyond our yard of wildlife fun lies a highway where the 70 mph limit is ignored. She doesn't know the danger lurking outside of her yard. She runs to the end of her freedom and quivers in anticipation when she sees the groundhogs emerge from under the gazebo. They've learned she can't get to them, and they inch ever closer, teasing her all the while. It is our job to keep her safe, in the same way parents keep their toddlers safe by child-proofing their homes. Not to ruin their fun but to keep danger at bay.

When we met Zoey we were vacationing in Southwestern Missouri during a trying time in our ministry. I'd found a place in between the small towns and hills of this lonesome part of the country that offered ministers a free stay. All we had to provide was transportation and our own food. It truly was a sanctuary located at the end of a dirt road where there was no Internet or cell service. The only entertainment offered was whatever DVDs we'd brought along. The nights were dark with only the moon to shadow the woods. Secluded and safe, it provided the respite we craved…and the companion we didn't know we needed.

She was trotting down the dirt road one afternoon while I was on the porch with a book in hand. I whistled, and she stopped momentarily then continued on her journey. I forgot about her until later that evening when we were watching a movie. Wayne was seated next to the window and jumped when she appeared, paws and face, in the frame. I recognized her and opened the door to her. We were careful not to let her into the no-pets-allowed house but gave her food and water, and she stayed. Wayne used tweezers the next day to pluck over fifty ticks off of her, and then we drove thirty miles to the closest Wal-Mart for flea shampoo, a leash, and a collar. We asked around, and no one knew where she'd come from. We let the kids play with her and gave into their pleas of, "We promise we will take care of her." We bathed her twice before bringing her home, and later in the week the vet declared her a little underweight but in otherwise perfect health.

Zoey now lives a life of luxury. We've guessed her to be half chocolate lab with her coloring and half beagle with her build. She has a comfy bed in three rooms in the house. She has a basket of toys in the living room and in the family room. The kids soon grew weary of feeding and walking her, so I am now mom to her too. She follows me around the house and checks on me when I'm out of sight. She likes to eat cut up zucchini when I'm cooking. She knows the sound of the popcorn rattling around in the old Mason jar when I pull it out for an evening snack. She sits at Wayne's feet and waits for him to finish a pint of Ben & Jerry's because she knows the container is hers to lick clean. We know what she likes and doesn't like. We know how she reacts in certain situations. We know she cannot be trusted in the house alone and will seek out trash cans or open kitchen cabinets (don't ask about the bag of flour she got into or the bag of Snickers she ate), so we confine her when we leave. The highlight of her day is when the mailman leaves a snack for her in the mail. She knows our bed is off-limits unless Wayne is out of town. She knows when we pull the suitcases out she won't see us for a few days. She cries when we leave and when we return. Her life is centered around us. We know what's best for her. She begs for grapes, but we refrain. She wants to sniff around the garage, but I make her stay in the house when I putter there because there are mouse traps and poisons.

I like to think God cares for me in the same way. He knows me. He created me. He knows what makes me happy and what makes me sad. He knows what is good for me and what I should stay away from. In the same way, the devil knows me. He is my enemy and has been studying me all of my life. He knows what makes me pause and what makes me stumble. The difference is that while God has guidelines in place to protect me and keep me safely in His fellowship because He loves me, the devil only wants to harm me because he hates everything God loves. He does not have my best interest in mind.

"Be sober, be vigilant; because your adversary the devil walks about like a roaring lion, seeking whom he may devour. Resist him, steadfast in the faith, knowing that the same sufferings are experienced by your brotherhood in the

world." 1 Peter 5:8-9 (NKJV)

He doesn't have your best interest in mind either. He is actively seeking whom he may devour. He wants no good for you at all. He is selfish and only desires to destroy you. He will use whatever means necessary to trip you and deceive you. Merriam-Webster.com defines *deceit* as "dishonest behavior" and as "behavior meant to trick and fool someone." He's a sneaky one. Yet while he is sneaky, he is also looking for weakness. If you've ever watched a nature show where the reality of the world is seen in all its bloody gore, then you know the predator always looks for the weakest animal to attack. He will get an antelope away from the pack or go for the baby. He doesn't try to go after the strongest one because he knows he won't be able to devour it. The devil does the same. He tries to get us when we are weak, tries to get us alone (one reason we need to be committed to a local church). Peter tells us to resist the devil and to be strong in our faith, knowing that the enemy is doing this to Christians all over the world. He's not just picking on you; he wants to destroy us all. This does not sound like someone we ought to give attention to. When you begin to understand his tactics you can better stand against him.

Do you wonder why he repeatedly tempts your weak areas? It's because he knows where your weaknesses lie.

He knows tempting me with a credit card and shopping mall isn't going to cause me to stumble. Shopping has never been that important to me, and I learned my credit card lessons, thanks to Dave Ramsey. Satan may choose to tempt me with food because he knows it's an issue for me. I've struggled daily with what I want to eat and what I actually eat for years. I've made changes in my life in order to maintain a healthy weight, giving up some of my favorite foods in exchange for healthier choices. I traded Vanilla Coke for water. Pizza is in my past. Bread is something I ignore unless I'm at an Indian or Italian restaurant.

I do still eat chocolate. I'm not stupid.

I've mentioned before that the Bible is a guidebook for life. Many people shun Christianity, saying it's a lot of rules they don't want to follow. As one who has served the Lord for over forty years (where did the time go?), I can assure you I've never looked at it as rules to follow. Just like the borders we have in place for Zoey, God has borders in place for my life to keep me safe. While I don't have much in common with my dog, we both make pleasing our master a priority in our lives. Zoey will wag her tail if I simply look at her across a room. She likes to burrow under my bed, and we can hear her tail thump-thump-thumping as we walk up the stairs. She is eager to be happy and to make me happy. My deepest desire is to please God. *Whatever You want, Lord* has been a prayer of my heart for years. Praying that turns the Bible from rules to follow to a how-to guide on growing closer to Him and maturing into the woman He desires me to be.

As a little girl I attended church alongside Candy and Cookie. Though not related to each other, they were friends, and at six years old I was sure my church was the coolest place in the world because of these two women and their delicious names. I'm still friends with Candy and can remember the day back in the 70s when we experienced a first together. She was my first Sunday school teacher, and I was in her first class. One of my favorite Bible verses is the first I ever memorized, taught to me in her class. It's underlined in my pocket New Testament by the not-so-steady hand of my six-year-old self:

"But be ye doers of the word, and not hearers only, deceiving your own selves." James 1:22 (KJV)

I've meditated on this verse for decades.

If we read the Bible but don't act on it, then we are being deceived. It's not enough to just go to church, sing a few songs, and listen to the word. We are to do it. I don't want to be caught in deception at the hands of the enemy or of my own volition. Read the Bible and let it change you into a doer. The more you read it and let it shape your life, you will desire to be closer to God, and the changes you make won't feel like something you have to do, but something you want to do. You will desire to please God.

Meditating on Scripture and memorizing it are two of the greatest acts we can do as Christians. The Bible tells us to hide the word in our hearts. This is so we have it when we need it for comfort, wisdom, direction, boldness, whatever circumstance we find ourselves in.

My mother told me for years that when I turned forty, things would start to change in my body, my eyesight being the first to go. I didn't believe her and made it to forty-three before things started getting a little blurred. A few years later and now I can't read anything without my reading glasses. I look at my hands and can no longer see my fingerprints unless I'm wearing the readers. Painting my nails is getting harder each year. Wayne leans in to give me a kiss, and I get dizzy (not from his rugged good looks either). Trying to tweeze my eyebrows is nearly impossible. To avoid a uni-brow I purchased an illuminated magnifying mirror. It's bigger than my head. To use it correctly I have to put my face right into the center of it, so close my nose almost brushes against it. The first time I got up close and personal with it, I may have screamed. And then I was hooked. When the skin is magnified you can see things you didn't know were there, and, let me tell you, there's a whole big mess going on. I got to tweezing and then realized the brows weren't the only thing needing plucked. *Gulp, a chin hair?* I'd thought they were the stuff of myths and legends. Not on my face. The light and the magnification brought clarity to the underworld in the mirror. It's the light that allows me to see what was going on and the mirror that showed it to me. In the same way, God's word is a light that shines behind the walls we build; it exposes the secret places in our hearts, the places He wants to renew. This is a continuing process. It won't be complete in our lives until we are in heaven with Him.

Whatever You want, Lord is a dangerous prayer. Surrender this way and He will take you seriously, and you may find yourself uncomfortable. He will also open doors and take you places you never imagined visiting.

"The steps of a good man are ordered by the Lord, And He delights in his way. Though he fall, he shall not be utterly cast down; For the Lord upholds him with His hand." Psalm 37:23-24 (NKJV)

If you are walking daily with the Lord and living to please Him alone, He will direct your path. He will guide you. He will catch you when you fall. He will keep you.

Questions for Reflection:

Do you have a special pet? Has your pet taught you anything about God?

In what areas do you find yourself tempted over and over again?

Do you memorize scripture?

What is the value in memorizing scripture?

What was the first verse you memorized?

What secret parts of your heart need to be changed?

-3-

Finding God's Will for Your Life

At a women's conference a few years ago I was invited to serve on the prayer team. At the appointed time during the service I joined several other ladies in front of the crowd of thousands of women and asked God to help me pray with them. I'm an introvert by nature, so this was out of my comfort zone. But I prayed *Go ahead, Lord, use me,* and I prayed with a guilt-ridden young woman named Alicia who couldn't forgive herself for cheating on her husband. Her story has stayed with me for years, and

I still pray for her by name. I prayed with a few other ladies, and then Julia approached me with excitement in her eyes. She stood boldly before me and said, "I told God I was going to come up here and whatever you tell me to do with my life is what I'm going to do."

That's not how it works.

I could have told her to sell everything she owned, donate the funds to a mission, and live on the streets or move to India and teach English as a second language. I looked her in the eyes and told her I would pray that God would lead her. She let me pray with her and then went straight into the line of another woman where I hope she received the same advice.

Haven't we all been there? I was in her shoes at one time. It was 1980-something, and I was the big-haired teen dressed in neon jelly shoes and wearing bright pink lip gloss. I attended church every Sunday morning, Sunday night, and Wednesday night, and Christian school Monday through Friday. I was never without my Lip Smackers, a can of Dr. Pepper, glitter nail polish, and the prayer, *What is Your will for my life, God? Please tell me.* I expected Him to answer with a booming voice and tell me everything about my future. I've learned He doesn't work that way. From a young age I was in tune with Him. I messed up along the way, as happens, but He was never far from my mind.

A lot has changed. My hair will never reach those heights again, and I've traded the Dr. Pepper for tea. I still have glittery nails though because...*sparkle*. One thing unchanged is the Bible is very clear on what God's will for our life is. Are you ready for this?

"Rejoice always, pray without ceasing, in everything give thanks; for this is the will of God in Christ Jesus for you." 1 Thessalonians 5:16-18 (NKJV)

Can it be that simple? Yes, and here's why. When you do those things and follow Him, He begins to reveal direction for your life. As a late teen I began to desire to be a pastor's wife. Looking back I wonder why I thought that would be fun. I've had good times, but I've also seen some of my darkest days while ministering to people in the church. It's better not to know what the future holds. The me I am today would probably tell the me of the 80s to purge that thought because some of it was too painful and I wouldn't wish it on anyone. I continued putting my relationship with the Lord first, and I believe it's kept me from bitterness. I've also kept my ability to laugh, and you wouldn't believe some of the things said to me by God's people.

One Sunday evening right before service was to start, Jill said, "You are so different from our former pastor's wife. I think I need you in smaller doses." What does someone do with a statement like that? I didn't know how to take it. I laugh at it now, but it still befuddles me.

A few more I remember are:

"You are not a pastor's wife, you're a preacher's wife."

"You need to stop breastfeeding your baby and start teaching Sunday school."

"I know how it feels to be a pastor's wife because my cousin is one and she told me."

"You need to be more involved in church activities."

"You need to smile more."

"You smile too much, no one can be that happy."

During one church business meeting a man in the front of the church started asking questions about me. "What does our pastor's wife do? She needs to be more involved in the church. I don't see her doing things. What does she do?" I slunk down in my seat out of embarrassment as our church secretary reminded him I had a job and children at home. I learned long ago that to be involved in ministry without His prompting is a recipe for disaster. Only when you do what He has asked, are you truly happy. If you are outside of His will, you can become quite miserable.

Have you found yourself asking God for hints of

your future?

Who will I marry?

When will I marry?

Will I have children?

Will I get the job promotion I want?

Should I get a dog or a cat?

Where should I go for lunch?

Should I move across the country?

Should I sponsor a child with Convoy of Hope's Feed One Program?

Should I take this job?

Should my son go to the pastor's son's birthday party? (No kidding, this happened.) Nicole, a mom from our church, called the day before the party and said Jesus told her Evan shouldn't come to the party. We were taking our son and some friends to a skate park, and we gave him a limit as to how many people he could invite. He didn't invite Evan's best friend, and Nicole was upset. The boys were getting in the car to leave when Nicole and Evan pulled up. Apparently Jesus changed His mind. (Jesus doesn't change His mind.)

Sometimes we need to use common sense when discerning God's desire for us. God leads us and will protect us from things we ought not to do, but other times it's just a matter of what we want to do. We can't pin the blame on Him when things don't go our way. Some things just aren't that important. Live and let Him lead.

Another passage I've found helpful when determining God's will for my life is found in Romans:

"Therefore, I urge you, brothers and sisters, in view of God's mercy, to offer your bodies as a living sacrifice, holy and pleasing to God—this is your true and proper worship. Do not conform to the pattern of this world, but be transformed by the renewing of your mind. Then you will be able to test and approve what God's will is—his good, pleasing and perfect will." Romans 12:1-2 (NIV)

It is an honorable thing to stand in church on Sunday morning, singing *I Surrender All* with hands upraised, but do you really mean it? When Monday starts with a missed alarm and dog vomit on the carpet and you want to curse. When Wednesday afternoon happy hour rolls around and your coworkers meet for drinks and things get a little out of control. When Friday night arrives and you find yourself at the theater watching *Fifty Shades of Whatever*. When Saturday morning finds you scrambling to pull together something to teach in Sunday school and you feel like you've got nothing...is it any wonder? You won't hear from God clearly if you're filling your life with things that are not pleasing to Him.

I once loaned a favorite out of print book to a friend. I received it back months later wrinkled, torn, and stained. It was nothing like it was when I'd entrusted her with it.

I imagine that's how God feels when He sees what belongs to Him returning to church on Sunday morning after chasing the world all week. Some don't even bother returning, yet still claim Him as their own as they walk the line between serving themselves and serving God. How can we expect to live a life full of peace and victory when we return to Him after letting ourselves be borrowed by our sinful nature all week? We flock to the altar and cry yet wonder why we aren't experiencing the victories we see in the lives of others around us. If you want to know God's will for your life, it's as simple as following the steps in the above verse.

"Offer your body as a living sacrifice, holy and pleasing to God—this is your true and proper worship."

This tells me that when I live my life and treat my body as a living sacrifice, when I pursue holiness and try to please God, He regards it as worship. Not just worship, but true and proper worship. There's no getting it wrong here. The end result of worship is being drawn near to Him. Getting closer to Him.

Hang on, what exactly is a living sacrifice?

The Old Testament taught us all about sacrificial offerings, and then Jesus came and died as a once-and-for-all sacrifice. I bet you thought the sacrificial thing was done. If you want to know God's will for your life, then it is so not done. Offering my body as a living sacrifice means I daily surrender my life to Him. I put aside my desires and ask that He use me for His purpose. I ask Him to take my life, use it, and if there's anything in me that needs to go, just say the word. It's not always an easy way to live, but then sacrifice isn't supposed to be easy. He will answer your prayer if you pray it in earnest.

The practice of Lent has been around since the fourth century. It has gone through several changes since then and has evolved into giving up something of your choosing between Ash Wednesday and Easter Sunday. Lent has grown in popularity in Christian circles in recent years with more participants each year. I generally see people give up Facebook or desserts for that short season. I've not participated in this particular fast because I'd rather live a sacrificial life every day instead of focusing on a few weeks of the year.

For me, sacrificial living has entered every aspect of my life. I had just settled into a new television series, when I heard Him whisper not to watch it anymore (and so went *Days of Our Lives*). Does it bother me to stop? Of course it does. Sacrifice isn't painless, but anytime we listen to Him, it benefits us. I was twenty when I first heard Him clearly speak to me along these lines. He asked me to stop watching R-rated movies. I hadn't seen more than a handful by then, but I took His words seriously. In 1991 I was invited to see the movie *The Doors* with an attractive and semi-famous man, and I ached as I walked away. The struggle was real: do I impress the guy or please the Lord? Even a decade later when *The Passion of the Christ* was released, I didn't see it. I figured God was likely okay with that one, but I didn't want to compromise with what He'd asked me to do.

Since then I've given up other things on my own, things I know do not bring glory to Him. I would rather my everyday be an offering to Him than just my Sunday. I would rather He look at my life and be pleased than do what pleases myself. I'd rather He accept my pursuit of holiness as worship. When it comes down to the end of life, in that moment between earth and eternity, it is only you and God. There is no one else. Your life, how you lived it, and whom you lived it for, are all that is going to matter.

Let's read those verses again in a different version:

"So here's what I want you to do, God helping you: Take your everyday, ordinary life—your sleeping, eating,

going-to-work, and walking-around life—and place it before God as an offering. Embracing what God does for you is the best thing you can do for him. Don't become so well-adjusted to your culture that you fit into it without even thinking. Instead, fix your attention on God. You'll be changed from the inside out. Readily recognize what he wants from you, and quickly respond to it. Unlike the culture around you, always dragging you down to its level of immaturity, God brings the best out of you, develops well-formed maturity in you. "Romans 12:1-2 (The Message)

Those words are His, not mine.

The King James tells us not to be conformed to the world. Merriam-Webster.com defines *conformed* as:

"To be similar or to be the same as something.

To obey or agree with something.

To do what other people do.

To behave in a way that is acceptable to most people."

We are supposed to be different. If we aren't different from the world, then what is the point? Why even bother calling ourselves Christians? Because it's a label we wear? Are we wearing it well?

Have you ever seen a recap of a Red Carpet event? The fashion experts critique the dresses and outfits of the attendees.

She wore it well.

What was she thinking?

Which designer do you think is more pleased? The one who heard affirming comments about his creation or the one who received less than flattering ones? Just like the designer spent time creating the clothing for these ladies to wear, our Father in heaven created you. He spent time thinking about you. You are the work of His hands.

"So God created mankind in his own image in the image of God He created them; male and female He created them." Genesis 1:27 (NIV)

When you take time to make something, you take pride in it. When I bake a cake to take to a dinner, I want everyone to know it's mine. I might handwrite what kind it is and put it next to my cake because I know my penmanship is easily distinguished. I worked hard on that ganache, and I want it to represent me well. In the same way, God wants us to represent Him well. If we wear the label of a Christian, but aren't any different than the world, doing what they do and acting as they act, then how well are we representing? Don't put the label on your life if you aren't willing to live it. The Bible is clear about how we are to deal with people who claim to be Christians but live otherwise. And it's a little scary.

"But now I am writing to you that you must not

associate with anyone who claims to be a brother or sister but is sexually immoral or greedy, an idolater or slanderer, a drunkard or swindler. Do not even eat with such people." 1 Corinthians 5:11 (NIV)

There are too many people claiming to be Christians yet living for themselves. A one-time prayer is not enough. Being a good person is not enough. Live the life worthy of your calling as a Christ-follower.

If we live daily as He wants us to, He will daily guide us, and we will have a clear understanding of what He wants for us. We will know His will. He will lead us in the way He wants us to go. His leading is sometimes as simple as a desire He gives us. Remember when I said I was a teenager when I felt the desire to be a pastor's wife? God put that desire there as a hint about His plans for my life. I never thought about being a missionary. I never considered a career in politics. Teaching was the major I chose in college because I had to pick one, but I knew I wasn't going to teach. The military wasn't something I was considering even though they tried to lure me with their ASVAB testing. My results said I'd make a good mortician. So not enticing. I don't even like touching live people, let alone dead ones. Managing a retail store didn't appeal to me. Being a businesswoman in a big city unnerved me. I did have a strong desire to be a wife and mother. He gently guides us. I love that about Him.

Following this line of thinking is not always easy. If it were, our churches would be full of mature Christians instead of aging people who haven't grown in decades. The devil will pester you like a sand flea at the beach when you start living this way. You will be ridiculed and heckled for your stand, even at the hand of other believers. I've had other ministry wives tell me my desire to live a pure life and be separate from the world is foolishness and isn't for them. This breaks my heart. God gave so much for us. Can't we live sacrificially for Him? It's for our own benefit.

What about you? Are you the Sunday morning Christian who can't get a handle on the rest of the week? Do you desire to be closer to Him but find the things of the world creeping in? Or are you stuck somewhere altogether different?

Questions for Reflection:

Are you still searching for God's will in your life?

What are some of your strengths? What are your interests or natural abilities? Do you think God can use these things you already have?

Do you seek God on a daily basis?

Do you find yourself compromising the standards God has asked of you?

How do you think God feels about that?

Do you think there is more He has to offer you?

-4-

Making Peace with Your Past

Trash pickup day is my favorite day of the week. I scurry around the house to empty all trashcans and get everything ready for Wayne to take it to the curb. I'm a firm believer in men's jobs and women's jobs. He can take the trash out. I will cook and clean. I want to get rid of the garbage; I just don't want to drag it down the driveway.

Let me tell you about Ben. His past is like a huge bag of garbage he refuses to take to the curb. He carries it around and shows it to everyone he meets. He brings it to church and carries it to the altar, dumps it on the floor, cries when he sees it but stuffs it all back into the bag and carries it home.

Everyone knows he carries garbage. He's told us all about it and has introduced us to it. We've seen it and smelled it. We've watched him be burdened under it and some of us have tried to help lighten the load, but he refuses. Almost every time I see Ben, he is dumping it out to show someone, and he's become the person others try to avoid. His audience is dwindling, and he is fighting for attention from anyone who will acknowledge the rotting bag he carries around.

I want to ask him if he's learned nothing from watching Elsa and Anna with his daughters. *Frozen* taught us more than just how to build a snowman. Let. It. Go.

The body needs half its weight in ounces of water every day just to function at a normal level. If you weigh one hundred fifty pounds, that's seventy-five ounces of water you should be drinking. I take this very seriously. And we all know the outcome of drinking a lot of water. I know where the closest restroom is within a ten-mile radius of home. I was dining Italian with some ladies from church and had to visit the restroom several times. On one visit I locked myself in the stall and was about to unzip when I felt someone staring at me. That is never a good feeling, but especially from within a locked stall. I looked between the cracks of the door to see a little girl peering at me. I moved to the side, and she moved so she could see me. As much as I tried to escape her line of vision, this curious little person kept finding me. I finally mustered up the most evil sounding voice I could and released a guttural sounding, "*Stop ittttttt.*" She ran so fast I thought I was watching a cartoon character dash away. When I emerged a few minutes later, I saw her from the corner of my eye. She was standing next to her table and pointing at me. "That's the one," I heard her say. I held my chin high and giggled as I made my way to my table. I wondered how she told her story—did she tell the truth? It's my hope she never peeks in on anyone again.

I want to do the same thing when I see Ben drag his trash to the altar and then, instead of leaving it there, take it home with him again. I want to shake his shoulders and say, *Stop ittttttt. Stop picking your smelly mess of a past up and let it go. Let God have it. Give it to Him once and for all.* He's counseled with people but won't allow it to be left behind. He carries it like a child with a security blanket. Ben will never receive the healing he is looking for until he stops carrying this around with him. He will never know true freedom because he holds onto his memories so tightly there isn't room for healing. He will never know how good his life could be if he would just let it go.

Are there things in your past that you can't escape? Many of us have experienced tragic events; some we can't bear to speak of, yet God sometimes does His best work though the tragic times. He can take the dirty and make it clean. He can take the broken pieces and make them whole. He brings our lives together one puzzle piece at a time, from all over and from unexpected places. When the picture of your life begins to appear, piece by piece, and you see the corners stretching into an image, you realize why a certain piece happened. The thing that confused you, the piece of life that broke your heart, the dark days when you barely climbed out of bed, they help complete the picture puzzle of you. You wouldn't be who you are without it all. Every moment of your life has shaped you into who you are today. What you do with the pieces is up to you. Will you let them be put together into a finished work others will want to see and know about?

We have scars. Some are internal and some external. Life hurts. It gets hard. I can look at my body and remember when I burned myself on the oven because I was trying to catch a pan of brownies, when I skinned my knee in a sixth grade bike wipe-out, and when I needed stitches on my forehead at an early age. There are scars to prove the pain. The wounds have healed, but the scars linger.

Internal wounds should be allowed to heal as well. Let God heal them. When you have an injury, you don't keep peeling off the scab; you protect it and let it heal. The same needs to happen with the things in your past you can't let go of. Let God heal. The scars remain, but scars are reminders of what happened. You can live with scars. You can testify that the wound healed, and you can help others deal with their wounds because of the scars. If Ben would let the healing happen and let the wounds scar, he could be an inspiration to others. Instead of avoiding him, people would turn to him for help because he's been there. Ben could minister to people who have been through the same things he experienced if he would allow God to complete this work in his life. He could impact people in ways you and I never could.

The reformed drug addict can minister to and encourage people who are in rehab in a way I never will be able to. The woman who had an abortion can talk freely with other women who carry the same weight because she shares their scars. The rape victim who has allowed God to heal her heart can give other victims hope. The abused wife can minister to others who share her past. The woman who lived through an affair yet saved her marriage can walk side by side with other women who have experienced the same thing. The adult who was abused as a child can help other adults deal with the insecurity in a way I never could attempt. I can give compassion, but they can give it from experience. We all have scars; it's what we do with them that matters.

There are things in your past that happened to you but not because of you. This is important to distinguish. You've nothing to be ashamed of, and you are not to blame for what was done to you. Quit beating yourself up for the actions of others. It was not your fault. You didn't ask for it, and there was nothing you could have done to stop it. Instead of hiding behind a wall of shame, remember to be thankful for where you are now. Look how far God has brought you. Do you see His hand guiding you from where you were to where you are now?

What if I told you there was a way to deal with the past as it happens and eliminate some scars altogether? Nothing would need to heal because you wouldn't allow it to injure you in the first place. Sometimes we carry scars as a result of being offended. Someone does something, says something, or neglects to do something, and we stir it until it burns.

Imagine beginning each day with a handful of white clay. You are able to mold it into whatever you want it to be, but at the end of the day it either hardens or stays pliable. What happens is up to you. Each time you let an offense linger in your mind, your clay hardens. Over time bitterness takes over, and your clay becomes hard as stone. When the hurts of your past become hard as stone and fill the garden of your present like gargoyles, they are harder to get rid of. Have you ever tried to lift a cement statue? It can't be done alone. It takes a lot of strong men and machinery to move it. If you deal with things as they happen, before they have a chance to harden, they are easier to let go of and easier to move out of your life.

The first step is to forgive. The entire gospel is centered on forgiveness. Without forgiveness, our faith is a lie. God forgives us when we ask and in turn asks that we forgive others. This is not an option. These are Jesus' words, not mine:

"For if you forgive other people when they sin against you, your heavenly Father will also forgive you. But if you do not forgive others their sins, your Father will not forgive your sins." Matthew 6:14-15 (NIV)

Let that sink in. It's frightening. If you hold onto unforgiveness, your heart is like a garden full of stone.

When you forgive, you begin to eliminate the stones holding you captive. Forgiveness is not about the other person. It is about you. This is the one time life is all about you. You can be completely selfish when you forgive others because it's what is best for you. Forgiveness is letting go and letting God handle it. In order to be able to minister to others, there has to be forgiveness. Holding onto offenses isn't allowing room in your life for dying to yourself in order to be more like Christ.

And that was the easy part. The second step is to love them and pray for them.

"But to you who are listening I say: Love your enemies, do good to those who hate you, bless those who curse you, pray for those who mistreat you." Luke 6:27-28 (NIV)

This is not what we want to hear. We feel better when we allow ourselves to wallow after we've been offended. It gives our flesh satisfaction to hope they'll get what's coming to them someday.

It hurts to pray for those who have mistreated us. They don't deserve it. I admit that there have been times I've wanted people to suffer for what they've done to me. Not in a life-altering way, but I would have liked them to be inconvenienced. Maybe sneeze for an hour or two straight, or get mosquito bites between their toes. What if everything they tasted from now on would have the flavor of liver and onions? Or what if they got stuck in an elevator for twelve hours with only Rod Stewart music to listen to? Uncomfortable is what I'd wish on them, but instead I'm asked to pray for them.

This is a recurring theme in the Bible as we are reminded again in Ephesians:

"And be kind to one another, tenderhearted, forgiving one another, even as God in Christ forgave you." Ephesians 4:32 (NKJV)

Be kind. Be tenderhearted. Be forgiving. And pray for them. It gets easier to pray for those who've wronged you the more you practice it. I admit the first few times I pray for someone who offends me or blatantly wrongs me, I do it through gritted teeth. It is in my head and on my lips, but hasn't quite reached my heart.. The more I do it, the easier it is to humble myself and think of the other person's best interests. After several times, I find I can pray a blessing over them without flinching, even if it's just a simple, *Lord, please help them to have a good day today. Bless them in their comings and goings and keep them safe.*

I'm working on letting things roll off of my back as soon as they happen. I recently donated a carload of items to a charity. The person working the donation center that day watched me struggle with box after box as I unloaded the car and carried them inside. She was more concerned with a stain on her pink ballet flats than with what I was doing. She never said a word as I stumbled with my load, but I sure said a lot of them as I drove away mumbling and complaining. God quickly shut my mouth when He reminded me how many times I neglected to help someone because my nails were wet. He reminded me to let it go and to pray for her. I prayed for her for the remainder of the day until I could do it without any negative feelings creeping in. What could have turned into me harboring ill against her was forever squelched. When I see her these days, I don't have any cynicism against her and don't remember her as she was on that day.

The startling truth about offense is that the person offended is usually the only one who remembers the interaction. They are the one with the problem. The person who wronged you in 2010 likely doesn't remember your name. You've been spending time and energy disliking them and remembering every bit of your interaction. Let it go.

I've been on both sides. I've been offended, and I've been the offender. If you have a mouth and a brain, then you've been both too. Early in our ministry we helped with the children's Christmas program at our church. On the morning of the presentation I saw Keith and his family for the first time in months, and in my excitement to see them I said, "It's so good to see you here. You aren't going to become the kind of people who only show up for special services, are you?"

What I'd meant as a lighthearted attempt to welcome them back, turned into a wall of offense. Months later another church member pulled me aside and told me how upset Keith was with me. It took me a while to remember what happened because I'd long forgotten our interaction. Keith, though, had spent months nurturing the stone statue in his yard. He showed it to others and even called former church staff to discuss my comments. I was oblivious to it all, but when I found out that everyone except me knew what was going on, I started to build a statue of my own.

This is how the enemy works. If he can pit us against each other, then he can destroy the church. I had to make a pointed effort to tear it down and let go of what I was harboring. We eventually got together, and I apologized for my offensive comments. Keith and his family even helped us through a difficult time a few years later.

The Bible speaks a lot about loving our enemies and about forgiving others. It doesn't mention liking people or trusting them again after they've hurt you. Just like the scars on our bodies remind us that we shouldn't grab the cookie sheet bare-handed, the experiences and times we've been hurt by people can serve as reminders that some can't be trusted with our hearts. There is nothing wrong with this as long as we've forgiven them and are not holding bitterness.

The church gossip who shared your private prayer request with others is not someone you should tell your secrets to.

The friend who stabbed you in the back repeatedly, even after asking for forgiveness, is probably not the person you should be spending the most time with.

The co-worker who made advances towards you after you told them you're happily married is not someone you should be alone with.

The pastor who told you to pay his cell phone bill because it was your duty is not someone whose teaching you should be under.

The church that teaches you to stop talking to your children if they attend church elsewhere is not a church teaching the Bible.

The boss who fires you for his own gain is not someone you wanted to work for anyway.

Life gets messy when people get involved, and it is

okay not to like everyone. Like and love are two different things. I can love a person who wronged me, but I don't have to like them. I can be kind to them and pray for them, but I don't have to be friends with them. Guard your heart. When someone offends you, let it go. When someone slights you, let it go. When someone puts their good ahead of yours, let it go.

Letting go doesn't mean becoming a doormat. If you are in an abusive relationship, please know that God is not at all a part of that. You can get out and get help. Let your scars heal and begin each day with a fresh handful of clay. Walking in forgiveness can be a way of life. God has so much He wants to do in your life and place in your hands, but He can't do it if your hands are full of offenses. Your relationship with the Lord will mature at speeds you can't imagine if you follow these truths.

Questions for Reflection:

Are there things in your past you can't escape from under the weight of? What are they?

Have you ever discussed them with anyone?

Is there anyone in your life you need to forgive?

Do you think forgiving will make a difference in your life?

In what areas can you minister to others using your own experiences?

Are you willing to be used?

Have you offended others?

Have you been forgiven by others?

How did each of these situations make you feel?

-5-

There's No Place Like Home

My love for *The Wizard of Oz* is no surprise to anyone who knows me. When Dorothy spoke the line, "There's no place like home," the filmmakers at MGM had no idea they'd just made one of the most recognizable quotes in movie history. Over seventy-five years later, it can still be found on tee shirts and wall plaques. We lived in the Midwest for a few years, and I had a refrigerator magnet with that famous quote on it, but the letter "t" in the first word had been rubbed off, and instead it read, "Here's no place like home." That magnet made me smile more often than not because I was homesick for Pennsylvania, the home of my heart. I never felt at home until we moved back, back to where we belonged.

Home is where I find safety and rest. It's a place of warmth, laughter, and peace. Home is where I belong and where others belong to me. It's a place of acceptance. No. Matter. What.

Perhaps home doesn't conjure the same thoughts for you because your home was never a happy place, but you desire a different experience for your own family.

Maybe your home was full of anger, and you want to break that cycle.

Maybe your home was split between two houses, and you never felt like you belonged at either.

Maybe your home was godless, and your desire is for Christ to be the center of your lives.

Maybe there was no time for you.

Maybe your home was filled with substance abuse.

Maybe your home was a lonely place, and you were left to fend for yourself.

Maybe your home was a place full of tension.

Maybe the weight of expectations kept you from being able to live.

You can change things. The unsavory circumstances of your past don't equate a future along the same path. It will be hard, but we all have hard days, no matter which path we've chosen. The Bible never promises an easy life, but when we have a relationship with Jesus, He walks with us in the hard days. I've never been fond of the *Footprints in the Sand* poem because I'd rather have Jesus walking alongside me through the ups and downs than carrying me. It's walking through the hard times that makes you stronger. When you're walking side by side with someone, you learn more about them. You can count on them to warn you when you're about to step on something or to get out of the way of a car traveling a little too fast. There's more to learn with someone walking beside you than when someone is carrying you. I want to learn how to navigate the rocky terrain on my own, so I can show others how to do the same.

Home is where our lives begin and occur. The daily stuff of life at home prepares us for what happens outside of the home. Home is my favorite place to be. The people are nice there, and the chocolate and tea are in abundance. I can spend all day in the kitchen because I love to cook. I sometimes think the only upper body workout I get is when I whip up a batch of the world's best brownies. The hours on my couch with a good book are some of my favorite moments. The furniture may be a little dusty, but I once heard Liz Curtis Higgs say that dust is a protective coating for fine furniture, so I'm good with the dust. My home speaks of who I am, and it's not perfect. We bought the worst house on our street. A lovely neighborhood but not such a lovely house. We thought we knew what we were getting into, a little cosmetic touch up here, a deep cleaning there, some fresh paint on the walls, and tearing down the wallpaper. When we purchased our house, we were thrilled that it passed inspection one hundred percent. This never happens. We thought it was a sign. We now think it was a conspiracy, and someone wasn't being honest.

Just like my house isn't perfect, I'm not perfect. I'm the same girl I've always been. In chatting with some college students, one posed the question, "What will I be like when I'm older?" I assured her she would be the same person she is now, just a different age. Her face would have some gentle lines, and her hair would start to grow silver strands. Her handwriting would be the same, but her clothes might be a little snug. She would think and feel the same way about things but would approach them differently as she's learned wisdom along the way. I still laugh at inappropriate times and probably always will. I stopped myself from laughing at a recent wedding I attended. As I was reading the program notes during a solemn part of the ceremony, what was supposed to read *exchanging of the vows* was printed as *exchanging of the vowels*. All I pictured was A-E-I-O-DO-U? I had to bite my tongue to keep quiet.

The truth about my house is it's always evolving. We put in a new gas line from the street to the house because there was a leak. Installed a new hot water heater because the one we had didn't work. We purchased a new water system for our well because the one that was here didn't filter the water. The entire heating system for the back part of our house was installed backwards, and it sounded like waves crashing on the shore when we turned it on. There is still so much wrong with this house, and I know if we tried to sell it today, it wouldn't pass inspection. The porch railings are falling apart, and I hesitate to have friends over because I don't want anyone to fall. I have grand plans on my Pinterest boards about what I'd do if money weren't an issue.

The same thing is true about my life. I've got plans and ideas of how my life in Christ should be, and I'm always evolving. The rooms in my house have changed paint color a time or two, the flooring is not the same as when we moved in, and the walls are cleaner. The family room in our lower level has reclaimed barn wood on the walls. Nice idea in theory, but whoever built this room hung the wood straight from the barn. I've spent hours scrubbing these walls from filth of all colors. I've joked that if these walls could speak, they would moo.

Even though it's a work in progress, I hope when people enter my home they feel peace. I hope they can sense we are lovers of Christ by what's around them. The things in our home reflect who we are. Are we seen as Christ followers when people enter our home and view what we have? As Wayne and I have attended auctions, I've begun to notice certain things about the lives of the people whose items are being sold. Our favorite auction to attend is one where the auctioneer brings estates to the auction house, and everything is for sale. People's lives are spilled out on the pavement for all to see. You can tell a lot about someone by looking through their belongings. At first I felt like I was being a little intrusive as I would search through the boxes. I've always been a rule follower, and it felt wrong, like going into the back room of a store with an *Employees Only* sign on the door. I have no qualms about it now and can dig through the boxes as if they were my own. Some things I've seen have shocked me, and others have disheartened me. I've seen boxes of pornographic magazines, trashy romance novels (A.K.A. porn for women – let's just call it what it is), sex toys, violent movies, games intended to summon spirits, and boxes of alcoholic beverages. On the opposing side I've seen boxes of Christian books by acclaimed preachers and well-worn Bibles, blankets, out of date décor, craft supplies, fabric, tools, and other regular household items. There are old books and toys, family pictures, and personal mail.

Some of these people were hoarders. Some were sentimental. Some were drowning in sin. Some were searching for answers. Some were stuck in time. Some enjoyed expensive things. Some liked the simple life. Some never threw anything away. Some loved God.

It is easy to tell who loved God and who never knew Him by what was in their house. When everything is laid out on the pavement for the world to see, will people know you were a follower of Christ? When the secret boxes you kept hidden are dumped out and on display, will they know? Maybe it's time to do some purging. Go through the rooms in your house and ask the Lord to show you what you need to get rid of. If it is coming between the two of you, then dump it. I've got a reputation for getting rid of stuff. I don't like to keep things I don't use, and if someone else needs what I have, I'll gladly pass it on. I've given away beds, an entire dining room suite, rocking chairs, clothing, even a car. You name it, and I've given it away. What good is it doing me to keep it in my attic? It's better if someone needs it and uses it. In the same way, what good is keeping something in your home that interrupts your relationship with God? If something is coming between the two of you, then get rid of it. Our life on this earth is very short. Don't fill it up with things that are in opposition of His word. Be careful what you let into your home, your life, and your heart.

When you and the people in your home live fully for God, choosing His will as your top priority, all other things will fall into place and your home will become a place of peace. I have witnessed this happen in my life, and it can happen in yours. The first step is to make sure you are right with God and that you are following His guidelines for your life. Not everything will be perfect because we are not capable of perfection in ourselves, but peace is such a lovely place to land when the world is full of unrest.

Here are some ways I've learned to make my home a peaceful place:

Love unconditionally. When we are loved by the people at home, it provides a blanket of comfort. We have bad days, and we mess up, yet knowing we are loved through it all gives us assurance that tomorrow will be better. This too shall pass.

Don't allow the people in your home to speak ill of each other. This was a huge one when my children were growing up. They'd come to me to complain about the other, and I always put a stop to it. There is a difference between concern and criticism. If they were concerned about the other, then it was fine to voice their opinion, but if they just wanted to tell me how stupid they thought the other was, it wasn't allowed to happen. Wayne and I made sure to speak highly of each other to our children so they would learn from our example.

Pay careful attention to what you're watching on television. I'll get into this more later, but know if you're letting violent or ungodly behavior be seen and heard on a regular basis, it will bring problems into your home.

Be careful whom you let into your home and know what they are doing when they are there. We've never allowed friends of the opposite sex to be in our kids' bedrooms. Too much can happen. Don't be the naïve parent who believes your child would never. Yes they would. It is your job to guard them from as many bad influences as you can. Keep your eyes and ears open. Interrupt them if necessary.

Get rid of the things that cause your relationship with the Lord to be put on pause. If there is something coming between you, then out it goes. There is nothing as important as your walk with Him.

Your home can be a place of rest and peace and of joy and fellowship. Learn what steps you need to take to make it home sweet home.

Questions for Reflection:

What does your home say about you?

In what ways have you improved your home?

What would you do to improve it if funds weren't an issue?

Are there things in your home you need to get rid of?

Are there things in your home that are coming between you and the Lord? What are they?

Do you have the strength to get rid of them?

The World's Best Brownies

¾ cup melted butter*
2 cups sugar
1.5 cups flour
½ cup cocoa powder
2 teaspoons vanilla extract (or chocolate extract)
4 eggs
1 cup of chocolate chips**
1 cup shredded coconut (optional)

Stir the melted butter and sugar together and then add in all other ingredients except for the chocolate chips and coconut.

Mix well and then stir in the chocolate chips and coconut.

Bake at 350 degrees for 35 minutes or until fork-tested done.

*If you are non-dairy, try coconut oil instead of butter
**Sometimes one cup of chocolate chips isn't enough, and if you are having one of those days, feel free to dump the whole bag in. It'll be fine. I've also used white chocolate chips and omitted the coconut.

-6-

WWJS

Do you remember the WWJD bracelets teenagers all over America wore in the 90s? We knew when we saw someone wearing one that they were in our club. They knew our Jesus. It was like a secret code, similar to when we're behind a car with a Jesus fish on it. We know we share something with that person. You'll never find a Jesus fish on my car because I prefer to stay under the radar when driving. If I cut someone off or run a red light, I don't want to be labeled a bad Christian. I also never wore a WWJD bracelet, but I am thinking of starting my own trend. WWJS: Where Would Jesus Shop? Maybe I will be able to get it printed on tees or socks, and it'll be the next big thing because somewhere in the "Rules of Being a Christian" there's a list of places where Christians shop and a list of places to avoid.

Chick-Fil-A is good because everyone knows they sell Jesus chicken and they're closed on the Lord's Day.

Hobby Lobby is also closed on the Lord's Day, and they sell a myriad of Christian-type things.

Forever 21 is good because they have John 3:16 on the bottom of their bags. Or are they hiding it down there?

In-N-Out is good because they have scripture on their packaging.

Altar'd State is good because they have scripture plaques mingled among their clothing, they play Christian music, and they have a book for prayer requests in their fitting room.

What if I told you I don't shop at any of those places? I don't avoid them, nor do I go out of my way to support them. If Chick-Fil-A is on my side of the road, I might stop in for an iced tea, but I don't eat fast food, so I probably wouldn't stop there or at In-N-Out. I'm not in junior clothes sizes, so I don't shop at Forever 21. I don't craft or decorate, so I don't visit Hobby Lobby, and although I love Altar'd State, the closest one is over two hours away.

Where do I shop?

I shop at Target because they have wide aisles, bright

lights, and an endless supply of my favorite tea. I think Jesus would shop there too, and if He were lucky there'd be a Starbucks inside where He could get a java chip Frappuccino because, yum. He'd stop at Home Depot for carpentry supplies. He'd order Bibles from Amazon because of their Prime Shipping program, and I believe He would even check out the latest Christian movie at the local theater.

He would be in the world, but not of the world. He would go where the people are. He would live life and not wonder if He was drinking milk from a Christian cow.

It was the spring of 1990 when I first indulged in a pint of Ben & Jerry's ice cream. I was a college student and my roommate and I walked to a deli and each purchased our own little bundle of delight. We sat on benches parallel to the soccer field, and I devoured my pint of strawberry ice cream while we talked about boys and watched the sun go down. We bonded that evening with the help of Ben & Jerry. I've had a love for their flavors ever since and mentioned it on Facebook recently. My thoughts put a fellow believer on the defensive, and they ridiculed me for supporting Ben & Jerry's liberal agenda.

Um, what? I'm just eating ice cream here. If anything, I was supporting my PMS with some aptly named

Chocolate Therapy.

It's so easy to point fingers. Let's think about this. Jesus doesn't care what kind of ice cream I eat. He's not facepalming my dessert choice. He's likely more concerned by the fact that someone else is making it their business and getting upset over my actions. It's ice cream, not sin. It could become sin if I allowed it to control me or if I became a glutton. Ben & Jerry and I have a true bond, so much so, that I named my backside: Left side Ben. Right side Jerry. My friends and family laugh about this, and when my daughter was eight she said, "Mom, you know how yours is Ben and Jerry? Well, mine is Star and Bucks." She said it in the middle of the ice cream aisle at the grocery store. I would much rather have her able to laugh with me and make memories instead of remembering all of the things we couldn't do because we were Christians.

When I go to Starbucks and order a hot tea from the barista who's having a bad day, and I have a chance to smile at her and tell her I like her haircut, doesn't that make Jesus happy? When the cashier at Target has a broken arm and I tell her I will pray for her, isn't that a better example of Christ than joining the latest #hashtag movement against the store? Who wants to be a Christian if we have to fear being verbally abused for shopping at

Target or for grabbing a latte at Starbucks?

Have you ever been around legalistic people? They are not a fun bunch. They are uptight and watch your every move, quickly pointing out the wrongs in your life yet not allowing the fruit of the spirit to be seen in their own life. These modern day Pharisees used to preach against playing cards. Not against playing a card game, but against the actual deck of cards. They reasoned the devil was in the cards because people gambled with them.

Dancing was another no-no. Remember Kevin Bacon in the 80s version of *Footloose*? I recently learned the movie was based on actual events, and the sweater the real life heroine wore is in a museum. Times were simpler in the 80s. Oreo's only came in one flavor, we had fudge-flavored bubble gum, and generic items were clearly marked with black print against white packaging. The Christian college I attended held student-sponsored off-campus dances, so they didn't have to be associated with providing questionable entertainment. Dancing to pop music was frowned on by most denominations, but those same churches would hold square dances in the basement fellowship hall.

The same people who refuse to go to the Olive Garden because there's a bar inside shop in the grocery store just steps away from the beer and wine. Should we stop shopping at Kroger because someone might see us walk down the wrong aisle? Satan delights in using these issues to take our focus off of the truth.

We knew a young lady who worked the concession booth at a movie theater. She was selling popcorn, soda, and candy bars to hungry movie goers yet was told by someone at her church that if Jesus came back while she was at work, she would be left behind. This left her bewildered because the Bible doesn't teach this. Things like these are false teachings, which lead to confusion and are very close to cult-like behavior.

My husband observed Lena walk through the sanctuary one morning. He was tucked in the sound booth, and she didn't know he was in the room. Lena was dressed in a plaid work shirt and oversized blue jeans, her hair tied back in a worn scarf, and she was carrying a bucket full of cleaning supplies. As she walked the length of the room, she prayed, "Lord, please forgive me just this once for wearing pants in the sanctuary. It will never happen again. I'm just too tired to go around to the other part of the building. Please forgive me."

This is not freedom in Christ. When he related the story to me, my heart ached for Lena. I wanted to tell her as long as her heart is right with God, He doesn't care what she wears in the sanctuary because He doesn't reside there. If her heart is right with Him, she won't wear anything displeasing to Him anywhere she goes. He is with her all the time, not just when she walks through the sanctuary. Honoring God with our dress is something we do daily, not only when we are in church.

He had a conversation with her a few weeks later. He was trying to explain grace to her because she'd never been taught it. "If I trip and fall in the parking lot after church on Sunday and swear, and Jesus returns at that moment, then I will still go with Him," he said. She looked bewildered, "You really think so?"

Can you imagine the pressure Lena was under? The pressure to be careful of every move because of her legalistic background? Who wants to live like that, knowing that –in her mind—at any moment she may slip up and if it's the wrong moment, she's doomed to hell?

God doesn't work like that. He gives us grace when we mess up. He forgives us. This doesn't mean we have a free pass to continue in sin. I knew a man who was addicted to pornography but refused to give it up, insisting it was covered by the blood of Jesus. Somewhere along the way he'd forgotten the words Jesus said to the woman about to be stoned, to leave her life of sin, to go, and sin no more. These words don't mean we will never sin again, but we are to turn from what is holding us captive. We are to walk away from it and not do it again. Apologizing is not the same as repenting. Repenting is walking away from something and not returning to it. If I were to repeatedly cheat on my husband and apologize each time yet continue to do it, am I really sorry? We may be able to fool people, but God sees the heart. Is this behavior worth risking eternity?

Grace is for the times we slip along the way. It covers us when we need it and turns us back to Christ because it is a God invention. Legalism ruins lives, divides churches, splits families, and turns people away from the Lord because it is man-made. The law is demanding, it pushes people away and closes people's ears. Grace covers us yet offers restitution in a way that isn't demeaning or overbearing. Grace simply changes us.

The businesses many avoid may be giving to causes you are strongly against but also have their hands out to charities. Target gives back to the local community. I've studied their giving board by the entrance and have been surprised to see who benefits from their generosity. The Home Depot gives to national organizations, and Amazon Smile gives to any non-profit of your choice, my church being one. Here's a secret: there are Christians working in these stores. If I don't shop there, am I denying a fellow believer a job?

Since Nike is the Greek goddess of victory and, therefore, a false god, we should probably burn our tees and sneakers. The Pepsi logo is said to represent Feng Shui, and the 80s were alive with controversy over the Procter and Gamble logo. The slope is treacherous. The only way we could avoid all of it, would be to buy a parcel of land, build our own house from wood we harvested, and plant our own self-sustaining garden. If we did that, then we would be secluding ourselves from the world. Where is the line drawn?

There are places, as Christians, we are to avoid because they are against God's Word. I'm not going to wear my Freedom in Christ badge and visit the local palm reader. I'm not stopping at Adult World on my way home from work. There are other places where the Holy Spirit has prompted me not to shop, but I won't question your walk with the Lord if you choose to because personal conviction is a different matter. If God reveals He doesn't want you to shop somewhere or if He tells you to quit doing something, then listen to Him. When He asked me to stop watching R-rated movies, I obeyed. It would be a sin for me to engage in the behavior He's asked me to give up. The key is to listen to His leading, but just because He tells you to give something up doesn't mean I have to give it up. The line of personal conviction and legalism meet right there, and we need to be careful not to confuse the two.

What if Jesus had never gone to speak with the woman at the well? If He'd listened to those who said associating with Samaritans was wrong for the Jewish people, Her life never would have been changed. Learn to listen for the voice of God, and He will guide you through life. Let Him have control, and the pressure will be off as you learn what freedom in Christ really is.

Questions for Reflection:

Have you found yourself boycotting businesses because Christians told you to?

Does your church teach grace or legalism? Do you understand the difference between the two?

What has the Holy Spirit convicted you of?

Do you know freedom in Christ? Describe what it means to you.

-7-

Let's Talk Social Media

It's true we don't connect like we used to. Even a century ago would have found us congregating on our front porches or spending an evening around a piano. Church was where we went to get to know people. If we had news to share, we'd write a letter with pen and paper and mail it, knowing it would take several days or weeks for the news to be shared. Radio and eventually television caused us to stay inside more and find entertainment on our own. We tuned into ourselves with our Walkmans in the 80s, and the 90s brought us our first home computers where we were introduced to the Internet. Few of us had mobile phones, and they were in bags we had to carry like an oversized purse. We only used them in emergencies, and even then, service was spotty. We soon found ourselves with online chat rooms where we made friends who seemed more authentic than some of the people we knew in real life. Our phones became small enough to carry in our pockets and then evolved into a device holding our world together. With one swipe, we can watch our favorite television shows or have access to endless information via the World Wide Web. We can join hashtag campaigns on social media, and we can share our #firstworldproblems with our friends. We are able to compete with others for attention on Instagram or Twitter. We can like and dislike, friend and un-friend. We have become socially alone with hundreds of friends, and we are bravest behind our screens. Things we would never say face-to-face are easily spouted online. Social media has become a wasteland of opinions, assumptions, and accusations yet is also a lifeline for many and can bring people together across the miles. There's an app for everything, and we've forgotten how to function on our own.

I've experienced both sides of Facebook. Colleen

asked her Facebook friends for advice on Facebook etiquette, so she could share it with her youth group. I replied, "Facebook isn't the place to air personal grievances, and swearing in general makes the user appear uneducated. Obscenities seem to have become filler adjectives. We've forgotten how to use the English language."

Maggie replied, "I swear all the time, it doesn't mean I'm uneducated. And people should be allowed to be sad when a loved one dies, there is never a problem grieving them."

I laughed as she unknowingly proved my point by confusing grieving with grievances.

If you've been on social media for any length of time you've come across these people. The ones who try to give a vague idea of their problems without naming names but knowing we know who or what they're talking about.

"I can't believe he did that to me again. It's my own fault for trusting him," posted the girlfriend who has been on/off with her beau for several years.

"She is wretched. I can't believe we share a last name," posted Jordan after her sister-in-law cancelled plans again.

"Someone won't buy me Maroon 5 tickets because we can't afford it, but he's going to the Penn State game this weekend," posted the wife who's been crushing on Adam Levine for years.

"Go ahead and say what you want to about me but remember what comes around goes around, and karma will come back and bite you in the rear," posted the mom who got into a yelling match at the PTA meeting about whether to sell hoagies or candles as a fundraiser.

"I can hold my head high and know I did nothing wrong," posted the woman whose husband left her.

"You can delete me as a friend, but it won't change what happened between us," posted one-half of former BFFs.

These types of grievances shouldn't be aired publicly. When we engage in this behavior, it does not honor the Lord and is not a good witness to others. It's okay to talk to our friends when we have a problem but talking to a friend is vastly different from shining the spotlight on someone (named or unnamed) in front of an audience. We need to remember our audience is not only the person we're angry with. This veiled attempt to vent without naming whom you're upset with is easily seen through. Just like a man with a bad comb-over, you aren't fooling anyone.

Social media has also given us a new definition of friendship, and sometimes the ones we call "friend" are anything but. Beth unloaded her feelings about her daughter in a public arena and was not happy when I sent her a private message reminding her that her words weren't reflective of her child but herself.

Her response was quick, and I could feel her hurt through her chosen words as she berated me for interfering. She interpreted my words as judgmental and accused me of being the kind of person who gives Christians a bad name. What little friendship we had, ended that day. I later learned her daughter had started using drugs, and she was trying to get her attention any way she could. Unfortunately there were several hundred others who witnessed her outrage, and my heart sank when I learned the truth.

When we choose words that are intended to hurt others or put others down in a public forum, we are showing who we are. There are two sides to every story, and while your friends might take your words as truth, hers will be doing the same thing. Some things are better left unsaid. We should filter our words through the mind of Christ and be careful what we post online. Don't post anything that you wouldn't want to be a breaking news headline on CNN. The little jabs we take at each other build walls one brick at a time. Once it is out there, it can never be taken back. Even if you've deleted it, someone has seen it or taken a screen shot of it. If it goes unsaid, there is no record of it. An actress who will remain unnamed was recently devastated to learn there were nude pictures of her making the rounds online. While I understand her outrage there is a lesson she could learn: If you don't have nude pictures taken, then no one will see any. Drama can be avoided by separating yourself from it. There has to be a happy medium in this world of Twitter, Instagram, Facebook, Periscope, Snapchat, Tumblr, Ello, and all of the other ones I'm not cool enough to know about. What can we do to make a difference in the online world? How can we use it to spread the love of God?

We can be the salt and light that the Bible teaches us to be. By rising above the drama and going deeper than the surface, we can outshine the darkness. There is good to be found in social media. Childhood friendships are rekindled. A friend from seventh-grade church camp who I never thought I'd see again shares updates of his life as a world-traveling missionary. College roommates too far away to have lunch with are able to share their lives. I've been able to contact authors and musicians, whose works have ministered to me, through their fan pages and thank them for their ministry. When my dad needed an emergency appendectomy, I was able to get immediate prayer from my friends on social media. I also know my own limits. I know I can't be trusted with a Twitter account because I've been known to eat my own words. Once something is Tweeted, it can't be reeled back in. Today I am struggling with my opinion on an unfinished job we paid someone to do. Everything in me wants to get online and shame this person for not following through with his work. I will remain silent on the issue because I don't want to be a re-tweeted embarrassment to my family. The Bible addresses remaining silent instead of letting our words rule us:

"Even fools are thought wise if they keep silent, and discerning if they hold their tongues." Proverbs 17:28 (NIV)

There have been plenty of times I wish I'd remained silent and even more times I'm glad social media wasn't at play during events in my life. Things I've thought and words I've spoken that shouldn't have. There are moments I'm glad there is no earthly record of. Social media has made it too easy to get a full glimpse into the lives of other people. Posting your every move opens you to scrutiny. An area newscaster recently lost her job over a post on social media and, while her words were fueled by grief, she was labeled racist, and her career instantly ended. We have to remember to be careful what we share online. Perhaps you attended a bachelorette party held in a bar. You didn't participate in anything shameful, but you posted pictures online, and there are people who attend your church who saw them. When you're leading worship on Sunday morning, how many people are unable to enter in because those images are burned into their minds? You may say it isn't their place to judge, but why do something that could cause others to wonder? When your words or pictures cause people to question your walk with God, it's time to evaluate if these activities are worth what you're projecting.

"Abstain from all appearance of evil." 1 Thessalonians 5:22 (KJV)

It's not any clearer than that. If it looks wrong, don't do it. If the pictures are questionable, don't post them. If the words are questionable, don't use them. If you don't put yourself into controversial situations, no one will be able to find controversy in your actions. People will still talk about you, they'll always find something to talk about if they look long enough. My husband and I moved to pastor a church out of state in 2004, and we were later told that the reason we moved was that we were getting a divorce (newsflash: still married). A few years later I learned, via the rumor mill, that the reason I'd lost weight was because I was sick and dying (newsflash: still alive). You're not going to get away from being a topic of conversation. Just be fabulous.

If you have children who have accounts online, and you do not have access to them you, you better address this today. Right now. Go ahead and do it, I'll wait. I have to put clothes in the dryer, so while you befriend your kids online, I will tend to my laundry.

You may trust your precious little ones, but believe me, they can get in over their heads very fast. We know to protect them from online predators and strangers, but they also need protection from themselves. The above rumors I shared were started by adults who should've known better. Teens and children can be much more cruel. Remember the movie *Mean Girls*? Imagine what that would've been like if social media had been at play? Your child can be sucked into both sides of the action, no matter how sweet they are. Don't be naïve. They need your participation in all areas of their lives.

Another important thing to remember when navigating the online social world is that not everything you read is true. I know, *gasp*. Deception is alive online and is being used to draw your attention from the important things of life. An inspiring quote you read while scrolling your newsfeed will never equal spending time in God's word. You cannot like or share something profound and think you've gotten your spiritual quota for the day. Nothing can replace quiet time with the Lord. It gives us what we need to determine lies from truth, and there are a lot of lies online. False teachers are leading people astray one "like" at a time. A self-proclaimed prophet recently posted, "I keep hearing the Lord say that sweatless wealth is on the way to the body of Christ." Her words were met with enthusiasm and not one person stood up for truth. God never said we could spend all day on the couch and watch the wealth pour in. Quite the opposite, as the Bible clearly tells us in 2 Thessalonians 3:10 that if we don't work, we don't eat. Working for what we have is part of the fallout from the original sin in the Garden of Eden. Be careful with what you allow yourself to agree with.

There is plenty of fun to be found online. You can be silly and represent Christ well. I love a good Facebook status. Here are some of mine from the past few years:

"Just did some serious organizing and got rid of a ton of junk. Okay, so maybe it was on Pinterest, but I'm still claiming exhaustion."

"Oh my stars, there was just a spider on me. I need therapy now."

"Bee just got suicidal in my perfectly brewed cup of tea #ruined."

"I always take the opportunity to kiss my husband when we go through a car wash. Even if he is wearing cowboy boots."

"At a party. Watching people eat the food I brought. No one has spit it out yet."

"So apparently sesame oil is a known laxative. Wish I'd known that before I used it in my stir-fry for lunch. #gottarun #brb."

"Maybe it's just me, but when a man drives up in a black BMW and asks where the local trailer park is, my mind begins to think sinister things. Especially after just walking past said trailer park and observing two people with bullet-proof vests on that were marked "agent" bursting into one of the homes."

"Sometimes when I've had my fill of tea for the day, and I want more, I just drink hot water. It's not that good."

"Package arrived today, and an hour later I got an email letting me know my order was processed for shipping. Nice to know they're on top of things."

"I have failed my daughter. She doesn't know what a square dance is. The Virginia Reel. Do-si-do. Allemande right. All join hands. Nothing."

"I may or may not have had more Nutella tonight than I should have."

"I could live very happily for the rest of my life without ever hearing a Jackson 5 Christmas song again."

"$49.99 boots at Payless. Oxymoron right there."

"My teenage self is jealous of my adult self sitting here in the front row of an Amy Grant concert."

"A friend just admitted she's never seen *The Princess Bride*. I replied, "Inconceivable," which of course she didn't get, and I told her she could borrow mine because no one should have to live like that."

"That awkward moment when you can't remember what your new car looks like or where you parked it."

"I think it would be awesome if, just once, someone would sing a Weird Al song for their audition on The Voice."

"Macy's is a little confused with their One-Day Sale that lasts forty-eight hours."

See? Funny stuff. There are things I've learned to stay away from. I keep my political views quiet. I don't engage in opinionated debates of any type. I refuse to disrespect my husband online because he's the one I chose for better or worse, and there's no quicker way to make it worse than to berate him publicly. Don't make life harder than it is. Think before you post and before you share things that should remain private. It's an easy trap to fall into; be stronger than the pull of it. Take advantage of privacy settings and friends or family lists. I have a *close friends* list I use on Facebook when I need to let those few people know important information. Facebook has an *unfollow* feature that allows you to remain friends with people but hide what they post so they don't show in your newsfeed. It's bliss. Put people you don't know or trust on the restricted setting. Be careful and be safe.

Questions for Reflection:

How will the world be a better place because of your tweet?

Does your online social media presence reflect Christ, or are you causing people to question which team you're on? Have you been berated or shamed online? What happened? How did you handle it?

Have you regretted any online interactions?

Do you think it's healthy to share everything?

-8-

Secrets, Part 2

Secret #4

Prayer Changes Things

If you think you can have a victorious Christian life without prayer, you are mistaken. Just like communication is needed in a marriage relationship to make it work, prayer is the communication needed in your life if you desire close fellowship with the Lord.

The basis of Christianity is relationship. It's what sets us apart from all other religions. In Christianity we have a relationship with a living God, but only if we communicate with Him. Just like any other relationship, it will thrive if we feed it and die if we starve it. God cares about you. He cares about your needs. He desires to communicate with you. You already know this. What's holding you back?

We've all heard preachers tell us to get into our prayer closets and spend hours crying to God until our prayers are answered, but we have laundry to do, diapers to change, dinner to cook, bills to pay, life to live. We can't hide our days away. There is a time and place for hours of uninterrupted prayer, but they aren't the norm. I've found I'm more often talking with Him on the go. Some of my deepest times of fellowship have been in the car because distractions of life, work, and family are left behind and I'm able to speak what's on my heart without interruption.

Have you wondered what it means to *"Pray continually,"* as stated in 1 Thessalonians 5:17?

I whisper prayers all day long, and I imagine this is what He likes the most, knowing that we are thinking of Him throughout our busyness. Just like when my daughter walks in the room, and I tell her I like her outfit, or when I'm at a restaurant and tell the waitress she's doing a great job, I can also tell God how much I like the sunrise (or sunset for non-morning people) that He painted or that I can see His handiwork in the softly falling snow.

Have you ever looked outside and been overwhelmed by the beauty? Tell the Creator. He loves to hear the praises of His people, and praise is not only a form of worship but also a form of prayer.

When I tell my daughter how nice she looks, I am getting nothing out of the conversation; it is a selfless act on my part. When I tell the waitress what a good job she's doing, my compliment is not benefitting me. It takes humility to lift others up, and it is solely for their good. Tell Him how thankful you are for the extra hour of sleep you had or for the baby who kept you from getting any sleep. Thank Him for the blankets that keep you warm and for the furnace barely getting by. Thank Him for the food you're eating even if it isn't what you were craving.

Have you ever been around someone who complains all the time? They are no fun to be with. Can you imagine all of the complaints God listens to everyday? Instead of looking at the things going wrong, why not search for the things going right? There is always something to be thankful for. The verses before and after 1 Thessalonians 5:17 remind us to rejoice always and to give thanks.

Today I am thankful for hummingbirds visiting the feeder hanging on the back porch and for the breeze tickling the wind chimes. I'm in awe of the shades of green outlined in the trees behind my house. I'm thankful for peace in the middle of my chaos.

I'm also thankful I get the opportunity to meet new people all the time. Not as thankful that I have a hard time remembering names. A few weeks ago I was introduced to a lady named Jandora, and that name I remember. It's the easy ones I have a hard time with.

One of the sweetest ladies I know is named Andrea, but she pronounces it with the emphasis on a different syllable than how it looks. I've known her since the 80s, and I can't remember how to say her name, and now with all these decades behind us, I'm too embarrassed to ask her the correct way to pronounce it. (Of course I am publicly confessing, and she will never let me forget it.) I've had friends tell me they make reminders of how to remember someone's name, but it's never worked for me. I have taken that idea and twisted it into something I can use. Aside from the names I have on Post-It Notes around the house (refrigerator, bathroom mirror, desk) reminding me to pray for the people listed, I have other prayer prompts.

A friend was having marriage problems, and her husband drove a blue truck. Whenever I saw a blue truck, I prayed for them. A glance at the clock at different times reminds me to pray for a friend whose phone number began with 655 or to pray for my son whose birth date is

10/17.

Doug and Carol are missionaries who asked our congregation to pray for them whenever we see bananas, a fruit in abundance where they minister, an easy prayer to remember in the produce aisle.

My husband hates having to stop at red lights. I've told him to pray for me while he waits at them, and it's changed his attitude towards them.

A pregnant belly reminds me to pray for friends struggling with infertility. Even seeing a face in the crowd resembling someone else prompts me to pray. Prayer prompts can be anywhere or anything. This is an easy way to improve your prayer life, and you will not be interrupting God. He is big enough to take care of the universe He created and give you personal attention at the same time.

Prayer can be an extended amount of time when you dig in and let God empty you of the excess. It can be a desperate cry in the midst of an emergency. Prayer can be the daily longing for Him to move in a situation too painful to speak of. Prayer can change lives and right wrongs. Prayer can restore families and calm storms.

For a few years I did some independent contractor work for various companies that would take me into stores to make sure items were on the shelves and being displayed properly. One early spring day my merchandising job took me to a Target store about thirty miles from home. We were living in Illinois at the time, and spring in the Midwest can lead to troublesome weather. I entered the store, leaving sunny skies behind, and soon heard the loud pounding of rain on the roof. The accompanying thunder was interrupted by the sound of distant tornado sirens.

I am a Northern chick. A Yankee. I didn't know tornado sirens existed until we took a pastorate in the Midwest. When I first heard them, they reminded me of the air raid sirens in the classic movies I watch. I wasn't sure whether to turn off the lights and close the blinds or take the kids to the basement. They quickly became a sound I dreaded. If I was home, I'd head downstairs, but Target didn't have a basement. I finished my work and meandered to the clothing where I chose some tees and shorts to try on. A friend later asked me why I was trying on clothes when the tornado sirens went off. I told her that if the roof blew off of the building, people wouldn't be concerned with me standing around in my underwear; there would be bigger problems. I took the clothes to the fitting room and passed several teen girls as a voice came over the loudspeaker. I didn't even know Target had a loudspeaker because the team members are all so well acquainted with their walkies. We were instructed to head to the back of the store because the National Weather Service issued a tornado watch. Cashiers were told to lock down their registers, and everyone needed to move. *Now!*

I collapsed onto the fitting room bench and began to cry. I prayed long and hard. I could hear the teen girls I'd passed complaining about the delay this was causing them, and I wanted to run out and shake sense into them, warning them that we could die here. Instead I prayed aloud. *"Jesus, You calmed a storm once before, please calm this storm now."*

Within minutes the same voice came over the speaker and told us we were free to go. I left the fitting room and ran to my car where I called home to learn the storm was taking the same route I needed to take. I spent the next hour at Barnes and Noble with chai and books because I figured if I was going to die, then that would be the perfect place for a tea-drinking book lover to do it. I later learned the tornado touched down less than a mile from Target. I thanked God for answering my desperate prayer and calming the storm.

I've seen many answers to prayer in my lifetime. A friend's foot straightened before my eyes, and I watched him walk without pain or use of the walker that he'd arrived to church with. My back was healed of scoliosis when I was in junior high, just one appointment away from being fitted for a back brace.

Another powerful answer to prayer is one my mother prayed during my high school years when I was in a relationship with a young man who my parents didn't approve of. They wouldn't even call him by name, instead referring to him as "the T word." Mom and Dad didn't go into all of the reasons why he wasn't a good choice but instead prayed for God to intervene and end the relationship. Not only did the relationship end, but his father accepted a job transfer, and the family moved to the far away land of Oregon. I never heard from him again.

In the same way parents want what's best for their children, God wants what's best for His children. He knows what we need and what we do not need. His answers sometimes are not what we want. I didn't want that relationship to end, but both my heavenly Father and my earthly parents knew it wasn't what was best for me. My heart ached, but if it hadn't ended, I probably wouldn't be where I am now, married to a man who loves God more than anything else and is serving in full-time ministry. God is faithful and always has our best interest in mind.

Secret #5

Her.

Can I be honest with you? I doubt there's a woman in the history of women who hasn't found herself looking at another woman and wishing for something she has.

I'm not speaking of admiration. I'm talking about the comparison game. We all play it.

I play it when I visit my sister and walk into her magazine-ready house. Everything is perfectly placed and spotless. Even her cats match the décor. I play it when I pick up my Saturday morning yard sale buddy, and even though I've told her sternly that there is to be no getting gorgeous at 6:30 a.m. (because I roll out of bed, throw my hair in a ponytail, and toss on my mom jeans), she still looks flawless. I look in the mirror after she climbs in the car and see the creases around my eyes and the grey peeking from my ponytail and wish for the younger me. It doesn't help when I hear, "Is this your mother?" as she's in conversation with someone.

I play the comparison game when I'm behind someone at Trader Joe's, and her behind is the behind I've always wanted. Her pants fit just so while mine feel a bit snugger just by looking at the chocolate babka in my cart.

I play it when a friend posts pictures of her tropical

vacation and I remember the only time I seem to get away is to visit friends or family.

I play it when friends are published, and I read my own words and convince myself they are drivel. I play it when I listen to a speaker give a flawless talk, and then trip over my own words when I do the announcements at church. I play it when I'm at lunch with a friend, and I can't concentrate on her words because her hair is curled perfectly while mine limply rests on my shoulders.

Comparison is exhausting.

The truth is nobody is perfect. Hannah Montana taught us that, and Miley Cyrus cemented it when she turned her back on her alter ego. None of us have it all together. We pick and choose our perfect selves from the women around us without realizing they're doing the same thing.

I've yet to meet a woman satisfied with herself and what she sees in the mirror. There is always someone better, stronger, smarter, prettier, skinnier, or younger. We can never be the ideal we have formed in our minds. The comparison game leads to self-pity and jealousy, both of which are in opposition to what God wants for us. Comparison and jealousy are so closely related I'm sure they share the same DNA. They deflate us with their lies and taunt us with pleasure, their words whispering we will never be enough. When we listen to them, we aren't able to hear what God thinks of us.

"For you created my inmost being; you knit me together in my mother's womb. I praise you because I am fearfully and wonderfully made; your works are wonderful, I know that full well. My frame was not hidden from you when I was made in the secret place, when I was woven together in the depths of the earth. Your eyes saw my unformed body; all the days ordained for me were written in your book before one of them came to be. How precious to me are your thoughts, God! How vast is the sum of them! Were I to count them, they would outnumber the grains of sand—when I awake, I am still with you." Psalm 139:13-18 (NIV)

Whoa. Did you see what I saw there? God made you. He knit you together in your mother's womb. He planned you. Have you ever spent time watching someone knit? They don't just sit down and do it; they follow a pattern. Without a pattern, their sweater may end up looking like a scarf. God took time planning you. He made you special, and there is no one else like you. He gave you some serious thought, and it's my guess that He doesn't like it when we question His decisions. Why do my legs bow so my knees won't touch? Why is my arch so high that my footprint looks more like an outline? Why did I get fingers so long they could play a cameo of the Wicked Witch of the West? I need to give Him some credit. It takes a lot of imagination to make each of us unique. I attended a painting class where the instructor gave our group a guided lesson on how to paint a sky, grass, and daisy masterpiece. Twenty-two of us painted the same picture, but each one was a little different. God continues to create people, and to keep coming up with ways to make us different proves His interest in each one of us. He got it right when He made you. There are many things about you that no one else can lay claim to. Comparing ourselves to others is a lie that keeps the truth hidden. While your neighbor may have a newer house with a kitchen that sparkles, she also has a much higher mortgage than you. Be thankful for what you have.

The lady I was behind at Trader Joe's probably doesn't enjoy food as much as I do, and I've learned that no amount of squats can satisfy like a piece of chocolate. My friend with the perfect hair lives with chronic pain and would gladly trade characteristics if she were able. My published friend endured a tragedy that spurred her writing career. We don't know the truth about anyone's life other than our own, so own your life. It's the only one you get, so learn to be happy in your body and with yourself.

Secret #6

God Loves You.

He truly does. With intensity you can't fathom.

"For I am convinced that neither death nor life, neither angels nor demons, neither the present nor the future, nor any powers, neither height nor depth, nor anything else in all creation, will be able to separate us from the love of God that is in Christ Jesus our Lord." Romans 8:38-39 (NIV)

He is crazy for you, and you can't escape it. His love shines on you like the sun shines on earth. You can't turn it off. It's always there. All you need do is bask in it and let it change you.

Emma attended our church when we were in youth ministry and for years had a hard time grasping that salvation was hers. She relentlessly questioned her past and raised her hand for salvation every Sunday morning. I used to giggle when she'd answer, "God's love," to every question my husband asked during his weekly lesson until I realized she was right. Her simple answer holds a lot of truth. *God's love* is the Bible in two words. God's love created the world. God's love delivered the Israelites from Egypt. God's love saved Noah and his family. God's love shut the mouths of the lions when Daniel was in their midst. God's love enabled Esther to save her people. God's love took Jonah to Nineveh. God's love chose an ordinary woman to carry His son. God's love caused John the Baptist to leap in Elizabeth's womb when greeted by a pregnant Mary. God's love allowed Jesus to be born humbly. God's love provided a way for us to be saved.

"For God so loved the world that He gave His only begotten Son, that whoever believes in Him should not perish but have everlasting life. For God did not send His Son into the world to condemn the world, but that the world through Him might be saved." John 3:16-17 (NKJV)

It really is all about God's love. The same love will encompass you if you accept it. It can heal your heart and change your world. Make the impossible possible. Remove the cloud that threatens your happiness. Fill your heart with joy. Give you peace you've never known. The same God who created you cares about you and loves you. You can't try to impress Him to gain favor. His. Love. Is. Right. There. Reach out and take it.

Questions for Reflection:

Are you satisfied with your prayer life?

Do you use prayer prompts? What are they?

If you don't have any prayer prompts, what are some that you think you could start to use?

How have you seen God answer your prayers?

Have you found yourself comparing yourself to other people?

Has this had a positive outcome or a negative one?

Do you know someone who appears to have it all together? Do you really think they do?

Are you comfortable knowing nothing you do will change how much God loves you?

Have you ever tried to earn His love?

Apple Cake

This is my most requested recipe, and it's so easy to make.

2 eggs
1 cup vegetable oil
2 cups white sugar
2 teaspoons cinnamon
½ teaspoon salt
1 teaspoon vanilla
1 teaspoon baking soda
2 cups flour
4 cups peeled and chopped apples
½ cup brown sugar
1 Tablespoon cinnamon

Preheat the oven to 350.

Grease and flour a 9x13 pan.

Beat the eggs and oil together until creamy and then beat in the sugar and vanilla; mix well.

Combine the flour, salt, baking soda, and cinnamon in a separate bowl. Add to the egg mixture and mix well. Batter will be very thick (I recommend using a wooden spoon). Fold in the apples until mixed well and spread in prepared pan.

Mix together the brown sugar and cinnamon and sprinkle it on top of the cake. Bake about 45 minutes or until it tests done.

This tastes better as it ages, so I generally make it the day before I plan to serve it.

-9-

Words

Some memories of my youth are cloudy. Others are more like a highlighted verse in my favorite Bible. It was a summer afternoon, and I had joined the neighborhood children to prepare a variety show. These were the 70s when *Donnie and Marie* ruled the airwaves and *The Partridge Family* taught us all we needed to know about performing. I wrote the puppet show scripts that would be the contribution from my sister and myself. While we were setting up our homemade stage, I started singing.

"You can't sing," a neighbor boy said. "When you sing it sounds like you're talking. You shouldn't even bother."

It's been nearly forty years, and I sometimes still hear his words. As a teenager there were times I'd think about performing and would hear them. If I let it, those words would be as alive in my mind today as they were then. It's taken years to silence his voice in my head. If I could ask him, he probably wouldn't remember saying them and would likely laugh it off as child's play. I've heard countless words affirming my vocal abilities, yet his opinion lingers. If nothing else, it's taught me the incredible power of the spoken word and how careful I must be with how I wield it. Overcoming negative things spoken into our lives is hard. Many people never get there and instead allow the soundtrack of those voices to play over and over. It can interfere with how God wants to use them, as it did with me.

Rebekah and I were enjoying lunch at an outdoor café when I began to share some words with her. "I've watched you for years and have been impressed with your maturity," I said.

"Stalking me, are you?" She took a sip of iced tea and laughed.

I shook my head. "You have so much wisdom, your character shines through, and I admire how you handle the hard things life has thrown at you recently."

She shrugged. "You don't see me when I'm alone."

"Girl, I'm trying to let you know you're doing a good job and others are noticing. Accept it."

Why did she have a hard time accepting my words? It's easy to let the negative things people speak over us impact us, but we need to let the good in.

Maybe you've heard words like these:

You're not good enough.

You're too fat.

You're too thin.

You're too old.

You're too young.

You don't have enough schooling.

You don't speak the language.

Who would want to listen to anything you have to say?

Why would God want to use you?

Do you remember what your past holds?

You're not qualified.

Something bad might happen if you try that.

What will your Aunt Becky think?

I can't believe you said that.

You can't do that.

You'll never succeed.

The voices and words fly at us from all directions and if we allow them, they can be the loudest voices heard.

We start to believe them. The untruth masquerades as truth if we listen to it long enough. A foolish utterance turns into a barbed wire fence we can't escape from. While we can't turn back and undo the damage, there are some things we can do to silence the voices.

Choose Who You Listen To.

Negativity attacks us constantly. I quit watching the news over a decade ago, and it changed my life. The daily reports of violence, destruction, war, crime, and even celebrity news threatened to drown me in a wave of fear. My thought life was dwelling on *The Latest Horrible Event*. The Bird Flu was sure to kill us, and if it didn't, then the outbreak of SARS in 2003 would. Most of Asia wore special masks to avoid contracting the illness.

Princess Diana died in a car accident after dinner in 1997, and footage of her accident aired often enough to make me wonder if my next restaurant meal would be my last. JFK Jr. died in a plane accident, which solidified my fear of flying. As I write we are mourning yet another mass shooting. I could tune in and watch every update, but I've learned it will only replace the fear that drifted away. Serial killers, ISIS, natural disasters. All of these are hyper-intensified by the media with the focus on them until the next big thing. The Internet is filled with stories and videos advising how to stay safe and not be a victim of a home invasion. We keep the windows locked because we're afraid to open them. I'd rather enjoy the breeze of the afternoon than board up the house. I'd rather sit on the porch and watch hummingbirds than lock myself inside. Wisdom is different than fear. Fear keeps us bound. Wisdom allows freedom while keeping watch. It's hard to find peace and happiness when the mind is filled with bad news. It takes less than five minutes online to learn all I need to about the world around me. By not filling my mind with the negative, I am able to do more.

What good did it do any of us to watch the O.J. Simpson trial or to watch every bit of information about President Bill Clinton and Monica? Hurricane Katrina destroyed numerous lives and left mass destruction, but the time we spent watching it didn't change anything.

The earthquake in Haiti, the Indonesian tsunami, the shootings in Columbine, Sandy Hook, and Orlando, if I let them, would fill me with fear. Pope Francis visited the United States recently and the news documented his every move. I didn't watch. His appearance on the other side of my state didn't have any impact on my life. What had an impact during the same time as his visit was spending time with my children, walking with a friend, reading my Bible, and going to church. Those are the things that will have a far greater impact on my life than what is going on in the world.

Quieting the words enables us to be still. It's in the stillness—the quiet—when we can hear the voice that truly matters. The voice of eternity speaks into our lives if we are silent and listen.

When lies from your past haunt your present what do you do about it? Are you choosing to listen to the lies or the truth God has spoken over you? His Word is full of promises. I've learned the best way to silence the lies and the father of them is by using the Bible. I've also been known to speak directly to him and tell him to leave me alone. There is nothing wrong with telling the devil to be quiet. He tries everything to get us off course. He tried it with Jesus in the wilderness.

"Then Jesus was led by the Spirit into the wilderness to be tempted by the devil. After fasting forty days and forty nights, he was hungry. The tempter came to him and said, "If you are the Son of God, tell these stones to become bread."

Jesus answered, "It is written: 'Man shall not live on bread alone, but on every word that comes from the mouth of God.'"

Then the devil took him to the holy city and had him stand on the highest point of the temple. "If you are the Son of God," he said, "throw yourself down. For it is written:

"'He will command his angels concerning you, and they will lift you up in their hands, so that you will not strike your foot against a stone.'"

Jesus answered him, "It is also written: 'Do not put the Lord your God to the test.'"

Again, the devil took him to a very high mountain and showed him all the kingdoms of the world and their splendor. "All this I will give you," he said, "if you will bow down and worship me."

Jesus said to him, "Away from me, Satan! For it is written: 'Worship the Lord your God, and serve him only.'" Then the devil left him, and angels came and attended him." (Matthew 4:1-11 NIV)

Jesus quieted him with the best words He knew, the Word of God. Jesus is our ultimate life example. He didn't give the devil any consideration. He was weak from fasting in the wilderness, but He stood firm. The moment we accept the Lord as our savior, we have access to the Father through Jesus, but we also receive the Holy Spirit, who is one third of the trinity, alive and living inside of us. He gives us power to fight the enemy when he comes at us with words of untruth and temptation. We have the power to quiet him through Jesus and through the Word of God.

Choose What You Listen To.

Our senses are incredible. Only God could create us to respond to our surroundings in such interesting ways. Have you ever caught a whiff of something on a passing breeze that takes you back in time? Maybe someone walked by you in a restaurant, and they were wearing your grandmother's favorite fragrance, and in that moment you were snuggled up next to her on the couch watching *The Parent Trap*.

In the fall of 1992 during our first year of marriage, we visited a little country church having an outdoor festival. The churchyard was filled with trees in the midst of spectacular color change. Some leaves had fallen to the ground and were littering the grass with orange, red, and yellow hues. Crafters were selling their wares, and in the center of it all was a big iron kettle over smoldering ashes. The smell of the bean soup cooking against the backdrop of the crisping leaves is embedded in my mind, and when I catch a certain autumn scent, I am twenty-three again and everything about that day envelops me with warm memories.

I've learned the sense of hearing can do the same thing. I've not had the sense of touch, taste, or sight take me back in time the way the senses of smell and hearing do. There are some songs that bring back memories I'd rather not have cluttering my mind. Memories of a bad break-up, a lonely time in college, or the job at the car dealership that I never really liked flood over me when I am unguarded.

Music is powerful and can touch us like nothing else, which is why God created it. Music can also be fun. If I'm busy with an important task, and the classic "Funkytown" starts to play, I am worthless for the next three and a half minutes. Words and music can linger for a lifetime. I've posted a lyric-of-the-day on Facebook several times, just a random line or two that pops into my mind during the course of the day. It's been everything from a "Zip-Ah-Dee-Doo-Dah" to "Joy to the World" (in May), but that's how music is meant to be. Wayne and I used to enjoy irritating our children by serenading them with praise songs from the seventies and eighties while on road trips.

While they're unfamiliar with the verses, we remember them even though we haven't heard them in decades. For this reason it is important to filter the music we allow into our minds. If we listen to sounds of darkness and sadness, then we will have a hard time coping when life throws us chaos. Don't get me wrong. I love happy pop music. I've set Wayne's ringtone to, "You're the One That I Want" because it makes me smile, but not all of it is as innocent. Some music is much darker and confusing.

I attended an ice-skating event a few years ago that was later televised, and while watching the TV version, I was entranced with one of the songs. I googled it and was about to purchase the album of ethereal music when I decided to read the lyrics first. What sounded lovely was not glorifying to God at all, quite the opposite in fact. If I'd allowed myself to listen to it, then it would have taken root deep inside and could have influenced me in ways that would not be beneficial to my Christian walk.

This is the way the devil works. If he can trick us into things that will bring us down, even using things that appear to be beautiful, then he is able to momentarily turn our focus from doing the work of the Lord. He makes the harmful appear innocent. Don't fall into his trap. Your heart is worth more than that.

I'm amazed when I'm able to sing a song I haven't heard in years the whole way through without any thought or hesitation. The church songs from my childhood find their way into my life, and the ones I appreciate most are nothing more than passages of scripture set to music.

"I have hidden your word in my heart that I might not sin against you." Psalm 119:11 (NIV)

Is there an easier way to memorize scripture than by singing it? The songs stay with you throughout your life and will minister to you when you need them.

"Thy word is a lamp unto my feet and a light unto my path," from Psalm 119:105 (KJV), is instantly recognized as more than just a verse in the Bible. It's likely you hummed along while reading it. I would much rather my mind be filled with His word and positive messages than things that will weigh heavily on my soul.

Choose Not to Listen To or Share Gossip.

I admit that I love me a good story. I think it's part of being a woman and our need to know things. I learned at an early age who to trust and who not to trust. The church prayer chain fell into the latter category. Stories change. It's part of life. When I was in third grade, we had our Sunday morning children's church service in the cool basement of the church. The adult-sized folding metal chairs easily slid across the tiled floor as we played the "secret" game. The teacher whispered a phrase into the ear of Joel who passed it to Jennifer who passed it to Lara, and so on until it reached the last student in the group. What was once, "Beth likes to eat tomatoes at the beach," ended up as, "better fries jelly no teeth."

Gossip is the same way, and the only thing we can do to stop it from happening is to avoid being part of it. My husband has gotten into the habit of not telling me church related information because he says I don't need to know. He's afraid if he tells me that Juanita complained to him about his clothing choice on Sunday, then it will make me think less of her, and he'd rather I get to know people on my own. He's a smart man. It is better for me not to know. A woman I've looked up to is known for her many godly character traits; however, I've witnessed her gossiping to others regularly. I wouldn't tell her my secrets. It's an easy trap to fall into, and I admit it is a weakness of mine.

I have a friend who teaches first grade and begins the school year announcing to the parents of her students, "I won't believe most of what your children tell me about you if you promise not to believe most of what they tell you about me." It's human nature to get the story wrong, especially if we don't see it with our own eyes.

My eyes told me the truth the night I went to a women's fellowship meeting at church, and Marcie threw up her shirt in front of the entire group, "Look! I got a tummy tuck!" My eyes also told me the truth a few years later when I joined a group of older women in a back room where they were changing clothes after being baptized. I turned around to see elderly Chloe wearing Nothing. At. All. I knew I'd just seen my wrinkly future. Sometimes, even if we see it for ourselves, we know we hold information we shouldn't. I can't change what I saw, and the image still haunts me.

I've learned some interesting things about myself from the mouths of gossips. One Sunday morning I spent some time at the altar during our worship service and was approached the following week by a concerned church member.

"Are you feeling okay?" She asked.

"I'm good," I answered. I must have looked perplexed because she continued.

"Mom said she heard you were having health issues."

Simply by spending some extra time with Jesus at the front of the church, I became a topic of conversation. I assured her I was fine, but grieved while wondering how many blessings the people watching and talking missed out on because they focused on me instead of on the Lord. People come up with crazy assumptions, and Christians aren't immune to being truth-benders. I don't watch Christian television or listen to nationally-known preachers on the radio. I'm blessed to live with my pastor, and the joke in my close circle is that I'm sleeping with my pastor. He's my favorite preacher, and I don't feel the need to binge all week on sermons from other sources. God and I have our time together, and I prefer to gather with my own body of believers. While I don't actively support other ministries, nor do I tear them down. I haven't figured out why the Christian community has no issue with destroying the reputation of pastors and leaders who they have never met. While we may not approve of a style of preaching or the way someone ministers, it is not our right to speak out against the ministry.

"Watch out for false prophets. They come to you in sheep's clothing, but inwardly they are ferocious wolves. By their fruit you will recognize them. Do people pick grapes from thorn bushes, or figs from thistles? Likewise, every good tree bears good fruit, but a bad tree bears bad fruit. A good tree cannot bear bad fruit, and a bad tree cannot bear good fruit. Every tree that does not bear good fruit is cut down and thrown into the fire. Thus, by their fruit you will recognize them." Matthew 7:15-20 (NIV)

God will take care of false teachers in His time. Instead of tearing down our brothers and sisters in Christ, we ought to lift them in prayer. Sometimes our words do more harm than good. The world is watching and listening. Why would they want to have anything to do with us, if we are constantly tearing each other apart?

Wayne and I were seated next to a table full of

women at our favorite restaurant. They were talking loud enough for us to hear them, and their conversation settled on their church and pastor. Nothing positive came from their mouths. I wanted to approach them and ask where they went to church, so I could tell them I would avoid their church at all costs, since they spoke so poorly of it. Instead I died a little inside with each negative thing they said.

There was plenty of unrest and gossip at one of the churches we served. One story to make the rounds came from Sheila who left the church, along with her family, and began to share her opinion of my husband with anyone who would listen. "There's a devil in that pulpit, and I will not go back until the devil is gone." Her words against my husband frightened me. Speaking this way about an anointed man of God will not end well. I wasn't surprised to learn that she was hospitalized the following week and had to undergo emergency surgery.

Spreading falsehoods about those in God-appointed leadership positions will never have a positive outcome. A similar situation a few years later left a man in our congregation with cancer. The God of the Old Testament who struck people down for lesser evils is the same God of today, and we need to be careful when speaking of those God has anointed. These are examples I've witnessed and it shakes me to think these situations may have been avoided simply by not spreading gossip. If you have a problem with someone, follow the Biblical route and go directly to the person in question to work it out.

Spreading negative opinions to anyone eager for a good story is simply being used as a tool of the enemy. If Christians would stop spreading gossip, think how many more people we could welcome into the kingdom.

Choose Your Own Words Carefully

We already know words can stay with us for a lifetime. What if we chose to be intentional with our words instead of allowing our mouths to rule our minds?

"The tongue has the power of life and death..." Proverbs 18:21a (NIV)

Have you spent time with someone who doesn't have a filter and says whatever bubbles to the surface without any thought of the aftermath? Patricia was one who was outspoken every time she entered the church doors. She never hesitated to state what was on her mind and how the church would be better if things were done her way. Everyone in leadership was a target of her arrows, particularly the pastor. One grueling Sunday afternoon, she approached me and apologized for her outburst.

"I don't know what comes over me. I just get so

worked up," she said.

I'd spent several years quietly listening to her rants, and this was the moment that God had been preparing me for.

"Set a guard over my mouth, Lord; keep watch over the door of my lips," I quoted from Psalm 141:3 (NIV). "I pray this before I leave the house, so I'm not quick to be rude with a slow cashier or with the server who spills my drink at a restaurant."

I shared with Patricia how it helped me filter my words and advised her to do the same. Remembering to use my words to build others up instead of tearing them down is something I have to make a conscious effort to do. It is human nature to react without thinking of the harm we may be doing. Perhaps if more of us prayed these words, the world would slowly become a better place.

When I thank the woman cleaning the public restroom at the Pennsylvania Turnpike rest stop, my words build her up. I was eating lunch with a friend and a woman with the cutest outfit passed through the line, I stopped her to tell her how much I liked her outfit. My words caused her to smile. Several weeks ago I noticed a woman who attends the same auction we do had changed her hair color, so I complimented her on it.

This is out of my comfort zone as an introvert, but when I take steps to speak positive words over someone, their countenance changes. Being intentional with our words can have a positive impact on another life.

Being intentional also means intentionally not saying words of a crude or vulgar nature. An aspiring author was in a Christian chat room and was being prompted by Jessie, another chat room member, to swear in her upcoming book. Jessie was an advocate for cursing and needed to be reassured by someone that it was permissible for a Christian to swear. Again, we look to God's word for answers.

"Do not let any unwholesome talk come out of your mouths, but only what is helpful for building others up according to their needs, that it may benefit those who listen.

Get rid of all bitterness, rage and anger, brawling and slander, along with every form of malice. Be kind and compassionate to one another, forgiving each other, just as in Christ God forgave you." Ephesians 4:29, 31-32 (NIV)

"Nor should there be obscenity, foolish talk or coarse joking, which are out of place, but rather thanksgiving. For of this you can be sure: No immoral, impure or greedy person—such a person is an idolater—has any inheritance in the kingdom of Christ and of God" Ephesians 5:4-5 (NIV)

The Bible clearly shows us what kind of language is

acceptable in the eyes of God. Curse words are not edifying in any way. If we are honest with ourselves, we can go so far as to say that even yelling, "Idiot!" when someone cuts us off in traffic is as bad as giving them the finger. I often stumble in this area and tend to tell the offender how stupid they are. While the word choices are wrong, the underlying problem is the attitude behind what we say. We are called to be different, to be set apart.

The Christian life isn't about us, it's about Christ working in us and changing us into who He wants us to be. It's a daily choice to pray, "Less of me, God, more of you," which is what we should be doing. Some days are easier than others, but He gives us grace and helps us when we stumble. Allowing God to have free reign in our lives opens the door to freedom, maturity, and peace.

Simple Things

Questions for Reflection:

Has anyone spoken words over you that have lasted a lifetime? Were they positive or negative?

Why are we able to accept negativity spoken over us more easily than the complementary?

Recall a time when someone spoke positivity into your life.

Are there any songs that remind you of things you'd rather not remember?

Are there songs that change your mood when you hear them?

Do you think it's important to listen to Christian music?

Have you been guilty of listening to or spreading gossip?

Share a story of a time when your words weren't as they should've been.

-10-

Friends

It's said that the relationship between husband and wife is the most intimate of all, and a Godly marriage should be a representation of how Jesus and the church (the bride of Christ) are seen. Nothing compares to the beauty of this intimacy, but friendship is a close second.

We need our girlfriends.

Who else but a girlfriend will tell you that your outdated mom jeans need replaced with something trendy? Only a girlfriend will listen to you rehash a workplace-related complaint for months. Husbands try to fix things. Girlfriends allow us to vent without trying to solve the problem. Girlfriends will tell us if our pants accentuate our thighs, whereas a wise husband will never admit to this. Girlfriends will sit through *Downton Abbey* with you. Girlfriends will rush to watch your children when you call early on Saturday morning with a hair emergency because the box of color you bought at the grocery store turned your hair orange instead of the strawberry blonde pictured on the front (I love my orange-haired friend!). Girlfriends will marathon watch *Anne of Green Gables* with you. Girlfriends will stay up late working on Pinterest crafts with you. Girlfriends will clean your house when you're too sick to get off of the couch. Girlfriends will hold your hair while you vomit after having surgery. Girlfriends will help you choose a wig after chemotherapy has destroyed your self-image. Girlfriends will help you eat the last bit of your birthday cake. Girlfriends will pull you out of bed, get you dressed, and force you to embrace reality after a bad breakup has immobilized you. Girlfriends will hold your hand when you bury your spouse. Girlfriends will buy you the mug you've been admiring when you don't think there's enough room in the cabinet for another one. Girlfriends will mail you chocolate when you're housebound with sick children. Girlfriends will dig a seventeen-year cicada out of your long curly hair when it gets stuck there...well, in theory they will. I failed at this in the summer of 1999. Girlfriends are invaluable.

Friends come and go throughout our lives. Friendships come in seasons. Some lasting a short time while others are in for the long haul. Some friendships last only when it's convenient, and others will move any obstacle to be together. Social media has made it easier to stay connected to those living far away, but some fade without any remedy. My earliest memories involve friends, most of whom I've lost contact with.

Gina and I had sleepovers in her Brady Bunch style house in the seventies. We stayed up late practicing our dance moves with an oversized pink satin pillow with John Travolta's *Saturday Night Fever* image painted on it. We tried to play pool but never managed to figure it out on our own.

Michelle and I used to ding-dong-ditch my fourth grade crush, Howard, before he broke my heart by moving to the other side of the world (Ohio). We'd hide in the bushes by his house and watch him open the door and look around. One glimpse was enough to make us shake the bushes with our silent laughter. Afterwards we'd play a rousing game of Stay Alive in her basement until it was time for me to bicycle home for dinner.

I met Julie on the first day of fifth grade. We were

climbing the stairs to go to class, both having transferred to Christian school at the same time. We passed notes to each other while our teacher read aloud from *The Lion, The Witch, and The Wardrobe* in his heavily accented voice. We shared secrets, scratch 'n sniff stickers, crushes on cute boys, and made friendship pins out of beads and safety pins for each other to wear on our shoes.

The neighborhood offered a different type of friend. My sister and I had playmates with whom we'd enjoy a game of hide-and-seek with after school, catch lightning bugs with in the summer, climb trees with in the fall, and sled ride with in the winter. These weren't deep relationships, we cared about each other but didn't share secrets; they were people we played with when we wanted a companion.

Junior high started a new era of friendships. Everything we knew about this type of relationship turned upside down when one week we signed our notes BFAAF (best friends always and forever), and the next we weren't speaking. These were the days of slumber parties and crushes. Of secrets told and then shared. Of changing bodies. Of popularity based on whose brand name was on the back pocket of your jeans. I haven't met anyone who remembers these days wistfully. High school was somewhat more settled. Our friendships deepened, as we learned who to trust. College brought new excitement to making friends; suddenly we were able to choose from people all over the country who were conveniently located in one small community. I found myself having lunch with friends from Colorado and dinner with friends from Louisiana and Florida. I'd take late night trips to the beach with people who just wanted to get away for a few hours. A roommate from Canada became a lifelong friend, while some of the others were eventually forgotten until we dusted off the yearbook to reminisce. I recently googled the cute football player only to find he's now bald and middle-aged.

Marriage and children made way for new friends, many called "friend" because there wasn't another name for it. The mom I sat next to at MOPS, the parents I sat with at story time at the library, the women I exchanged coupons with while waiting for preschool to dismiss for the day, and the ladies I shared nursery duty with once a month at church.

Friends travel in and out of our lives, and over time we learn to choose our friends carefully. We get to know them before trusting them with our hearts. The tentative steps of a guarded heart lead us towards lasting relationships where we are comfortable navigating deep waters together. Perhaps you've learned this lesson the hard way and have been burned by someone who wasn't who you thought they were. There is no rhyme or reason to why some relationships last and others wither. Friendship is a gift. Sometimes the simple gifts are the best, and a true friend can be closer to your heart than family. True friends can be trusted; they rejoice when you succeed and want the best for you. Friendship isn't jealous or envious, nor is it manipulative. A friend accepts you for who you are and doesn't try to mold you into who they think you should be. Jesus chose His friends carefully, and I find myself looking at His example. His twelve disciples were his traveling companions, and among them He found his closest three friends. These were His inner-circle, the people He trusted most. These were the ones He turned to when weary and needing away from the crowds. The ones He asked to pray with Him.

We've gotten comfortable in the mindset of touting Jesus as a friend of sinners. We sing about it and boast about it, as we say we're going to hang out at the bar because Jesus did. Unfortunately we are twisting scripture to something inaccurate. Jesus wasn't friends with sinners (people living daily in sin, not saved by grace, the unsaved); he was friendly to them. The Pharisees of the day who referred to Him as a friend of sinners meant it as an insult. Jesus came to seek and save those who are lost.

He met with the sinners and ministered to them in their time of need. He shared a meal with them. He saw them, had compassion on them, and showed them there was more to life than the way they were living. He did not immerse Himself in their world and share in their lifestyle. Jesus was sinless, so He didn't do what the sinners did; instead He influenced them and caused them to change. He was a humble leader who related to people where they were. He gave of Himself to them but didn't share in their worldly activities, nor did He share His personal life with them. He saved His personal life for His closest friends, yet even He experienced friendship trouble with those He trusted.

Judas betrayed Him.

Peter denied Him.

Peter, James, and John fell asleep when He asked for prayer.

Thomas doubted Him when He appeared after the resurrection.

These were his closest friends. Who among us has never had friendship trouble?

The Bible has plenty to say about every kind of relationship, including friendship. A starting place for how to choose friends wisely comes from a verse I've only heard quoted in reference to dating relationships.

"Do not be unequally yoked together with unbelievers. For what fellowship has righteousness with lawlessness? And what communion has light with darkness?" 2 Corinthians 6:14 (NKJV)

The New Living Translation says it this way:

"Don't team up with those who are unbelievers. How can righteousness be a partner with wickedness? How can light live with darkness?"

Our friends are the people we choose to spend most of our time with, the ones we laugh with and lean on when times get hard. It makes sense that they believe the same way we do. If we, as believers, surround ourselves with friends who don't have the Holy Spirit dwelling within them, how can we live as strong for the Lord as we desire? As Christian women, there will be people we are acquainted with whom we influence, but these should not be our closest friends. Our closest friends should be those who urge us to grow closer to the Lord, make right choices, and help others do the same. Someone in right standing with God will be able to counsel in accordance to His word and will speak words of truth into our lives. Someone without biblical standards will not be able to offer Godly advice. Learn the difference, as Jesus did, between friendship and being friendly.

Learning who is trustworthy is essential when it

comes to finding a good friend. I've experienced the bitterness of opening my heart too soon to a person who I thought I could trust, and my words were used against me. Being in ministry has added a different dynamic to my friendships. We've learned through experience that the first people to pursue us at a new church are the ones who we need to watch out for.

Naomi and Fred were the first to greet us at a church where we'd just accepted a position. Then within a week, Naomi was lying to both my husband and me about things we separately said. She was using our own words against us, trying to divide us. Fred verbally attacked my husband at a church board meeting and said, "I could run this place better than you," among other choice words. Yet the day we met them, they were as sweet as the apple pie they gave us.

Jesus has proven Himself to be the truest friend there is. He never lets us down. He always listens and always cares. He is trustworthy, never sharing the secrets of the heart. He is faithful and always loves us.

If you haven't invited Him to be part of your life, I would love to introduce you to Him. His life and death story is found in the pages of Matthew, Mark, Luke, and John. I believe that these words are true and that there is both a heaven and a hell. If it weren't so, there would be no need for a savior.

Your choices determine where you will spend eternity. The biggest decision you will ever make is choosing to believe or not believe. Choosing to follow Jesus gives you access to heaven, and by rejecting Him, you choose an eternity in hell. The reason hell exists is because God cannot be in the presence of sin.

When Adam and Eve took the first bite of forbidden fruit in the Garden of Eden, they opened the door for all humanity to sin. We are born sinners and Jesus came to forgive us of our sin.

When we accept Him, we are given the gift of eternal life in Heaven. We are to turn our backs on our sinful lifestyle and instead live a life glorifying to God. We still make mistakes, but God forgives us when we ask. God allows us the choice to sin or to repent, therefore determining our fate. If you are ready to invite Him into your life, then find a church in your area or pray this simple prayer:

"Jesus, I believe you are the Son of God, born to live on this earth and die for my sin. I believe you rose from the dead and are waiting for me to come to heaven to be with you. I accept your love and ask you to forgive me for the times I've sinned. I know I am not perfect, and I ask you to help me live as you did."

If you just prayed that prayer, please pick up the phone and call the friend who gave you this book. She wants to celebrate with you.

Questions for Reflection:

What is the earliest friendship you remember?

Who has been your friend the longest?

When was the last time you made a new friend?

What qualities do you look for in a friend?

Have you ever had to end a friendship?

In what ways have you experienced the friendship of Jesus?

-11-

Your Local Church Needs You

Far too often I've heard Christians admit to not attending church. When questioned they toss excuses:

"Church isn't relevant to my life."

"The music is too loud."

"My kids aren't being spiritually fed."

"There's no depth."

"All they want is money."

"There are cliques at church."

"The preaching is too deep."

"The preaching is too shallow."

"I like contemporary worship."

"The pastor preaches from the NIV."

Let's not leave out the universal excuse, "The church is full of hypocrites."

What do we expect to find in church? Churches are full of imperfect people. We've discussed the difficulties in marriage and friendship. Why do we expect church to be any different? There will never be a perfect church, as long as earth is filled with imperfect people. Some churches are better than others, but the bottom line is that church is a building where flawed people come together to learn about God and to grow in Christ. It's where we celebrate life events and mourn loss together. Where strangers become closer than family. Where we can correct and be corrected. Where we are encouraged to spread our wings and blossom in the areas God has gifted us.

Vivian and Bill were on a quest to find the perfect church. They would stay somewhere for a few years until the pastor offended them, and then they'd be on their way to the next church. Bill asked for a meeting with the pastor after church one Sunday.

"I want my tithes and offerings back," he said. "And Vivian is deleting all of the documents she created on the computer in the media room. We don't like the way things have been going here."

The pastor was stunned. "Let me check the office and see if today's offering is still here."

Before he could stand up, Bill said, "I mean all of my tithes and offerings, since we started attending here."

The pastor had to explain why he was unable to return five years of donations and later had to scramble to create new documents after Vivian completed her dismantling of the media files.

This is just one example of what this pastor has had to deal with during his years of ministry, and if anyone had reason to quit, it was he. Pastors are regularly leaving the ministry because of the demands of church-goers. Your local church needs your support, and your pastor needs your support.

"Let us hold unswervingly to the hope we profess, for he who promised is faithful. And let us consider how we may spur one another on toward love and good deeds, not giving up meeting together, as some are in the habit of doing, but encouraging one another—and all the more as you see the Day approaching." Hebrews 10:23-25 (NIV)

We need each other. Not only to further the gospel but to encourage one another. There are things I've learned in the church environment that I never could have learned elsewhere.

I've learned how to worship in a corporate setting. I've learned how to serve, sometimes alongside difficult people. I've learned we all have spiritual gifts, and not one is better than another. I've learned when people use their spiritual gifts, it doesn't make them a better Christian or even a mature Christian. I've learned some of the greatest work is done behind the scenes. I've learned how to give. I've learned everyone has a testimony. I've learned how to pray. I've learned not be swayed by every new doctrinal fad meandering the Christian road. I've learned my gifts and talents are not your gifts and talents, and it takes all of us working together to build the kingdom of God.

Your church needs you. There are things you can give your church community that I can't. You're an expert at lawn care? I've never cut a blade of grass in my life. You love to work with children and babies? I loved working with my own children and babies yet have never been fond of children who don't share my DNA; but put me in a room with some teenagers, and I'm happy as can be. You love to drive? You'd be perfect for picking up people who are unable to drive themselves to church.

Several years ago, a man in our church approached my husband with a ministry idea he'd been praying about. Scott is an accountant and thought it might be beneficial to the church body if he volunteered his ability to do tax returns. He envisioned being able to provide free tax return processing for not only our church members but for our entire community. The first year he completed two returns. After just a few years, this number grew to over two hundred and thirty tax returns, a quarter of which were from people in our church. This ministry, the idea of one man who was willing to use the gifts God blessed him with, has gone beyond the walls of our church to a people in need. It's growing at a rate of about one hundred persons per year. And while it is a free service done by Scott and a team of volunteers, some of the recipients have given back to the ministry. This year $2,200 was donated, and Scott gives it to the church building fund. He has moments of frustration during tax season and spends time working on the tax returns of strangers while we are tucked in for the night, but he wouldn't change it for anything. Scott is providing a service that I wouldn't attempt.

A church in our area has a wood ministry. Our winters in Central Pennsylvania are unpredictable but always cold. This church has access to wooded property, and men volunteer to cut down trees and chop them into logs for firewood. People across the area benefit from the selflessness of these believers whose gift warms homes all winter. God can use your ideas, training, and talents. The church is a good place to think outside of the box.

Church has taught me how to give. God doesn't need our money. We don't give to line His pockets; we give out of obedience. Giving is more for us than for Him. The more we are obedient to Him in all areas of our lives, the more He pours blessings on us. God promises to supply our needs, but we sometimes get confused as to what our needs are. We need food and water. We don't need Doritos and Vitamin Water. There is a big difference. We need shelter from the elements. We don't need a five-thousand square foot home by the sea. (I mean, really….we don't.) When we learn to be satisfied with the simple, the rice and beans or the basement apartment, we realize the blessings we have.

While God doesn't need our money, the local church does. If you aren't being obedient in giving back some of what the Lord has blessed you with financially (it all comes from Him whether we like it or not), then you are perhaps hindering the work He wishes to do in your community and in your life. If you hold back, your church can't support missionaries, pay its bills, and possibly pay its pastors. Too many pastors are forced to be bi-vocational because people in their churches aren't giving regularly. A pastor has a stressful job; it isn't right to add stress to his life by causing him to try to make ends meet while you sit in your comfy Sunday morning seat, belly anticipating the meal you've been dreaming about during the sermon. Pastors are leaving the ministry in droves, and some of this could be avoided if the church gave recklessly. What if, instead of placing a bill or two in the offering basket, you wrote God into the budget and gave Him what He's asked for? Have you not learned by now that He will take care of you? Your local church needs you to be a giver and not just a receiver.

Going to church has taught me to think for myself. For decades I've watched people chase the latest movements and change their belief system based on what's trendy or relevant. I've been sick and have had people tell me not to claim the sickness. "You're not sick," another pastor's wife told me. "Don't claim it."

I had a cold, my nose was stuffed, and I had chills and a cough. My hand was full of used tissues as she patted me on the back and told me I was definitely not sick. I wanted to sneeze on her but instead kept my mouth shut. A few years later she was hospitalized after being in a serious car accident. My first thought was to visit her and tell her to get out of that room because she wasn't injured. As the church, we need to watch our words. Her admonishment to me could have been devastating to a new believer. We need to worry less about being culturally relevant and more about being Biblically sound and quit making Christianity harder than it is. Your local church needs believers who understand God's word and live it.

Having grown up in church, I've been privy to some beautiful things. I've witnessed healing and have seen restoration of marriages. I've also seen the ugly side of things and have been scarred by hurts that can't be seen. Many people give up on church because they've been hurt by the church, yet they don't understand that it wasn't the church that hurt them. The church itself cannot hurt anyone. Hurt is caused by people, some in leadership and some in self-labeled leadership. One of the biggest life lessons I've learned has been how to stand up for myself, and specifically, at the hands of good church people. I've encountered people who could cause Hannibal Lecter to lose his 2003 American Film Institute title of "#1 Movie Villain of All Time."

Giving up church was never an option for me, no matter how many cruel people I met along the way. I may have skipped a Sunday or two, calling my husband while on the drive to church, "I just can't do it today," I said, turning the car around to head home.

Once in a while we would see the fruits of our labor

when the villain would take off their mask and allow the Lord to work in their life. Unfortunately most of the villains were cemented in their ways and never moved on from their initial salvation experience. We watched them live lives that they thought were victorious, only to be abandoned by their friends and family. What they labeled persecution was merely the result of their behavior. We need to be careful to represent Christ well. The world is watching; we need to be the light.

Some people behave so brutally that the hurt they cause can be crippling. If this is where you are, please understand that God did not do this to you, and He does not condone it. He doesn't work this way. He is not selfish or cruel. Some people who claim to be His are indeed not. I've long heard of people from all walks of life who claim to see a bright light during a near death experience. Remember this: the flames of hell shine brightly too. Not everyone who claims to be a Christian is one. If you've left church because of physical, sexual, or mental abuse, I applaud you. I also beg you to find another one. There are good churches. I've been in both the good and the rotten. There are people who will walk beside you as you learn to heal. Take time to find a body of believers. Make sure the church preaches from the entire Bible. Look for strong leadership in both staff and in volunteer positions. If you are currently attending a church where abuse is happening, I urge you to leave immediately. You don't have to stay in any relationship where you are being abused. God does not want this for you, no matter who says it's okay. It. Is. Not. Okay. Find someone who will listen to you and will help.

If you are someone who finds fault in every church you attend and seem to have the same issues time after time, I urge you to consider that maybe the church isn't the problem. Sometimes all that's needed is a long look in the mirror.

Find a church where you can be used and where you can learn but remember to keep your focus on Jesus. People will always let you down, but He never will.

Questions for Reflection:

What comes to mind when you hear the word *church*?

Do you know what your spiritual gifts are?

Have you heard people talk about believing in things you find questionable?

Have you seen prayers answered?

Do you know someone who's abandoned church?

-12-

Once Upon A Time

Once upon a time you were born. Somebody loved you and took care of you. Somebody taught you to use a spoon, to talk, and to walk. As a toddler, someone took you to a park and bought you a balloon. In the midst of the excitement, you tripped, the balloon slipped through your fingers and floated to the sky. Your tears were evidence of hurt in your heart as you watched the balloon fade into the blue. You learned the feeling of loss, and your eyes opened as a little innocence was swept away. You continued to lose innocence as you grew and bloomed into who you are today. Nothing is as it was when we were little. Sometimes the simple things are the hardest lessons learned, but this is life, and we've only got one chance at getting it right. Each day is a new page waiting to be written, and we can't hang onto anyone else to get through our own stories. We will either end victoriously or lose it all. God promised to give us what we need to get through each day. People often say that God won't give us more than we can handle, but this is not true; the verse that has been twisted, actually says,

"No temptation has overtaken you except what is common to mankind. And God is faithful; he will not let you be tempted beyond what you can bear. But when you are tempted, he will also provide a way out so that you can endure it." I Corinthians 10:13 (NIV)

This deals with temptation, not trials or stressful situations. God won't allow us to be tempted beyond our capabilities, and He will always provide an escape. The Bible never says we won't see hard times or be buried under so much that we can't see our way out. What God does is give us what we need to get through each day. When we give our lives to Him and surrender to His will, His Spirit comes to live inside us. We nurture this through worship, prayer, and reading the Bible. We then begin to display the fruit of the Spirit, which should be evident in anyone who claims to belong to Christ. These should have an active role in our lives, and when nurtured, they are deeply rooted, helping us stand firm. They give us comfort and remind us there is more to life than what we have physically experienced.

"The acts of the flesh are obvious: sexual immorality, impurity and debauchery; idolatry and witchcraft; hatred, discord, jealousy, fits of rage, selfish ambition, dissensions, factions and envy; drunkenness, orgies, and the like. I warn you, as I did before, that those who live like this will not inherit the kingdom of God.

But the fruit of the Spirit is love, joy, peace, forbearance, kindness, goodness, faithfulness, gentleness and self-control. Against such things there is no law. Those who belong to Christ Jesus have crucified the flesh with its passions and desires. Since we live by the Spirit, let us keep in step with the Spirit." (Galatians 5:19-25 NIV)

Let's take a quick look at the fruit.

Love

Who doesn't want love? I want it, lots of it. Love is something we can never have enough of, nor can we ever give enough away. Love has more songs and stories than any other subject. Love is overused and understated. God gives us a never-ending supply; He is constantly showering us with it, and even if we get it from no one else, His love is enough to sustain a parched heart. It's easy to show love to people we love but isn't so easy to show it to the unlovable. I'm a people-watcher. In any given situation, I am likely focused on everything around me while listening to conversations I shouldn't be privy to and wondering why certain clothing decisions were made. I've seen love in action at a meet-and-greet where a Christian entertainer hopped from stage to embrace a cross-dresser. I've watched the church van driver give up his Sunday mornings in order to provide a ride to church for those unable to get there on their own. I've observed the couple who minister weekly to inmates, sacrificing their time and resources to invest in the lives of those who many have turned away from. I admit, I didn't pay much attention in school because I was focused on everything around me, but one of my Christian school teachers once taught us this definition of love, "Love is choosing the highest good for God, others, and yourself," which is based on C.S. Lewis' words, "Love is unselfishly choosing for another's highest good." Love doesn't look around to see what others think. Love acts. Love reflects Christ.

Joy

Joy is likely my favorite fruit (besides strawberries, which are pretty perfect and made even better after God gave us chocolate to dip them in). If you've ever lost your joy, then you understand. There was a time when I felt the joy being squeezed out of me by people wanting to mold me into something I wasn't. Through the ministry of Liz Curtis Higgs on VHS (don't say it, I know I'm aging myself), I was able to rekindle my joy. I have a friend named Joy who embodies the name. She is never without a smile, even when she is falling apart on the inside. Her countenance radiates the joy of the Lord. I call her *Joyful* because it's what she is. Joy is what we lean on when everything is in disarray. Joy enables us to smile in the middle of tragedy. Happiness and joy are not the same thing; you can be happy and not have joy, but joy is nestled inside. Nehemiah taught the Israelites, "*The joy of the Lord is my strength.*" Nehemiah 8:10 (NIV)

Joy is what filled Tara, allowing her to smile during her last days of breast cancer. Joy is what filled Jenna as she lived through years of abuse. Joy is what Andrea bubbles with, as she shuffles her children to appointments located hours from home for multiple medical issues. Andrea carries a heavy burden but doesn't show it. Joy carries her through.

Peace

The world has been crying for peace for centuries. The peace from God is what I feel when all around me is in chaos. It assures me everything will be all right. When mom has a day filled with diapers, tears, fevers, no sleep, and no help, she can still have peace in her heart. I remember days of constant chatter from little ones, so loud it made me dizzy. I found time for peaceful moments even if it was after they were tucked away for the night. Peace can be found in a teacup with the aroma of cinnamon and spice. I've found peace on country roads with the windows down and the music up. Peace can be found in prayer. Peace is in a text from a friend reminding me this too will pass. Peace dances in snowflakes, it's in memories of traditions, and is in the middle of a silent night. I crave peace and will hunt for it in the same way I rummage for chocolate.

Patience

When we are at peace, we are able to have patience. Patience is something I learned to never pray for. I spent time studying the 1 Corinthians 13 poster on my bedroom wall in my early twenties and decided to pray the chapter in order to be more loving. I never made it past praying for patience. The next few months spiraled downward as I lost my job, a relationship ended, and other smaller events stabbed my heart. It's a prayer I've yet to repeat, but God has given me patience as I've matured in Him. The closer we get to Him, the more we become like Him, and He is the author of patience. Patience is waiting in long grocery lines without muttering. Patience is cleaning up the dog mess when housebreaking them. Patience is repeating a task until it's right. Patience is starting over. Patience is potty training. Patience is being married and staying married. Patience is what God shows us. Every. Single. Day. Patience is waiting to hear His voice and knowing His time is not our time.

Kindness

Kindness is appreciated when it's shown to us. It's going out of our way to help someone. It moves us from comfort. Kindness is responding to harsh words with a gentle tone. Kindness is what Jesus showed the woman at the well and what He did when he reattached an ear cut off by a disciple. Kindness was Jesus acknowledging the sinner on the cross next to Him. Kindness fuels me to make my husband a morning cup of tea when he asks. Kindness is waiting to hold a door for someone and letting them enter before you. Kindness is being polite when you finally talk to a real person after playing tic-tac-toe on your phone when dialing 1-800-Help-Me. Kindness is keeping my mouth shut when I have a million things I could say. Kindness is bending to talk with a child or sitting to speak with the elderly. Kindness is treating others how we want to be treated.

Goodness

Goodness is part of purity. If the opposite of good is

evil, then goodness is what we want. When something is good, it lacks evil. Goodness is safe and harmless. God is good. We are to behave in a way reflective of Him. We are to be good. We are not to sin. It's hard, and while we will never be sinless, our sinful times should be fewer as we grow in our faith. When something is good, we want more of it. We should be so full of goodness that others want to be near us in hopes it'll be contagious.

Faithfulness

Faithfulness isn't one we hear of often in reference to anyone other than God Himself, but we sure do hear of unfaithfulness. Whether it be in a marriage relationship, a friendship, or a church membership situation. There are faithful people and unfaithful people. The faithful are the ones we can count on. Faithfulness is solid. It isn't going anywhere. Niagara Falls faithfully spills water over the edges. The tides in the ocean faithfully pull and push. The sun and moon faithfully rise and fall. Our hearts faithfully pump blood through our bodies. It isn't until something goes wrong, that we consider faithfulness. It's trusted and just there. God is faithful in this way. We know He is always caring for us and always loving us. We know He listens when we pray. We know He will provide for our needs. He is faithful. We are to mirror this and be faithful at home and at work. Be faithful to those you love and those who love you. Be faithful in giving to your church and in church attendance. Be faithful in parenting and in caring for others.

Gentleness

With gentleness is how I want to be treated by God when I mess up. I want His hand to gently guide me to where He wants me. Gentle correction is better than the alternative. Gentleness can be lived out by our actions and words. *"A gentle answer turns away wrath."* Proverbs 15:1 (NIV)

Gentleness walks alongside peace; when we are gentle, peace abounds. When we are harsh, anger flares. Gentleness is a quiet spirit, an unwavering calm. Gentleness is how we handle a newborn while marveling in her. Gentleness is carefully walking the fine china department at Macy's. Gentleness will not harm anything in its path.

Self-control

Self-control. *Sigh.* Do we have to talk about this one? Self-control is what we want, but when faced with a situation in need of it, it's hard to find. Self-control keeps us from overeating, even when tiramisu is on the dessert menu. Self-control is walking away from the iPhone 7 when you have a perfectly good iPhone 5 in your pocket. Self-control is maintaining your composure when someone backs into your car in the mall parking lot. Self-control is reading your Bible and taking time to pray. Self-control is discipline, and living a disciplined life is a big part of being a Christian. Self-control is surrendering every area of your life to God and not giving into the lust of the flesh. Self-control is trusting He has a plan and will complete it in His time. Self-control is giving up and being in control at the same time. It's not easy but it's worth it.

Attributes of the Spirit

These attributes that we see in Jesus and God should be evident in our lives. Each of them has pieces of the others intertwined. Where there is patience, there is self-control. You'll find love in kindness. Gentleness and peace work together. Love and faithfulness are simpatico. Joy and goodness are kindred spirits. They work together to deepen our faith and mature us, each causes our desires to take a back seat and instead focus on those around us. When we are weak in one area, the others step in to build it back up. God amazes me with how He works in our lives. The Christian life is not for the selfish but for the humble and strong. People who know us should see these virtues in our lives. We should be known as the patient one or the good one. Has anyone ever described you as peaceful? I want to be known as having self-control and gentleness. Let's be kind and faithful.

Once upon a time you had a hard life. Heartache has touched all of us. You are not alone. Every moment is part of your story. Live it well and have a happily ever after.

Questions for Reflection:

Have you witnessed the fruit of the Spirit in action in someone's life?

Which fruit is hardest for you to display?

Do you think we should have these represented in our daily lives?

How can we build them up?

Special Thanks....

It's said a writer works alone, and I've spent many hours alone with this book, however, I couldn't have done it without the cheerleaders and helpers in my life. I'm so grateful for those who have come alongside and encouraged me to continue.

If I've forgotten someone, I apologize, know that you're tucked in my heart.

Thank you to the endorsers and launch team who took time to read and give feedback: Marjie Tourville, Doree Donaldson, Liz Hoffman, Sonya Wilson, Leigh Powers, Nicole Bingaman, Rebekah Sanders, Dawn Kauffman, Rene Tourville, Krista Knapp, Rosemarie Noftz, Kristin Odell, Becky Dougherty, Christa Fowler, Jennifer Sprankle, Tammy Lundgren, and Rebecca Reynolds.

Courtney DiTrilio, your editing magic worked wonders!

Adessa Holden, I truly could not have done this without you. Your heart to help and to serve has melted me time and again. You are such a blessing.

Andrea Nagle, Cindy Loven, Sharon Neveu, Scott Seifer, Joy Bickle, Melissa Avesian, Candy VanBriggle, Dawn Clark, Arline Grabill, Lisa Madeira, Jodi Jones, Sharon Poole, you've all helped inspire me in different ways. Thank you.

Micah and Bethany Marshall and Troy Ferguson, thank you for taking the cover I imagined and bringing it to life.

Marsha Seymour, Cherie Lee, Maria Finley, I couldn't survive without your friendship. Julie Blackburn, thirty-seven years since we met and I'm so thankful for you.

My family for encouraging me.

Wayne, Michael, and Carly, you are my dream come true.

Thank you, Lord, for the work you've done in me and for the work you're doing through me. I love you.

About the Author

Suzanne is a pastor's wife, mom, and lover of tea, old movies, and chocolate. She believes life is too short for mediocre food and tries to find the humor in every situation. She lives in Pennsylvania with her husband, daughter, and Zoey the wonder dog. To read more from Suzanne, visit www.notenoughchocolate.blogspot.com.

All proceeds from *Simple Things* goes to Convoy: Women, a division of Convoy of Hope whose goal is to empower women in impoverished nations. Teaching them how to build better lives for their families and giving them hope through Jesus in the process.

Made in the USA
San Bernardino, CA
26 February 2018